Bitcoin: The Inverse of Clown World

Knut Svanholm and Luke de Wolf

Foreword by Giacomo Zucco

Edited by Mel Shilling

21M

Lemniscate Media

Edited by Mel Shilling.

To our friends, families, and all the guests of the Freedom Footprint Show.

Contents

Foreword

There are various writers known for their humorous, light, and engaging writing styles, but sometimes their content falls short, appearing shallow, disorganized, or misleading. Conversely, some authors excel in delivering concise, comprehensive, and accurate insights to their readers; however, their writing style might come off as overly pedantic, pretentious, or even sleep-inducing. Then, there is *Knut Svanholm* at the intersection. Wait: *I mean the good kind of intersection!* Entertaining style and great content! There's also the bad kind of intersection: boring style and banal content, but that's not very common among Bitcoin-related authors, to be fair.

In the realm of wannabe authors, there exist those perfectionist dreamers who pour their hearts and souls into grand ambitions of creating "The Single, Perfect, Indispensable, Timeless Book" they will never end up finishing (I'm afraid I may be part of this sad cohort, even if Knut made many efforts to help me get out of it, so far unsuccessfully). Then there exist other, more reliable authors who are very prolific, publishing many, many books that are just disposable, single-use collections of extemporaneous blog posts or transcribed conference talks. Then, there is Knut Svanholm at the intersection. Wait: *I mean the good one, again!*

After enjoying all the previous (funny yet insightful) books by this (prolific yet perfectionist) author, I was both humbled and thrilled when Knut asked me to write the foreword to his latest effort (this time a four-hand effort, co-authored with *Luke de Wolf*, more on him later). And since many of our very, very pleasant conversations tend to end up with the drawing of some Venn diagram (like the one that you will find in the "Pendulum" chapter of this very book), it only seemed fitting to begin such a preface with one. Admittedly, it's a 4-set diagram, not the typical 3-set kind I tend to aesthetically prefer...but still, I know he will appreciate ending up at the center of it.

I first interacted with Luke de Wolf during the recording of my entertaining (at least for me, but I hope for listeners as well) incursions in *The Freedom Footprint Show*, the podcast he created with Knut, and has very successfully run for quite some time at this point. Luke is not as loquacious as Knut and most definitely not as talkative as me, but over those several episodes, I ended up appreciating his role in capturing, provoking, stimulating, and somehow even directing Knut's polyhedric streams of consciousness. I have to say, after reading *Bitcoin: The Inverse of Clown World*, I can clearly see his beneficial and complementary fingerprints (or, better still, footprints) all over the place.

Now, since both Knut and Luke like to indulge in Bitcoin numerology (as evident from the date they chose to launch their podcast), I'll leave you to **the 21 reasons you should read this book**!

1. Just like the podcast, this book was released on Infinity Day, August 21st!

2. If you are reading my foreword to this book, it's very likely you already spent some of your precious sats to purchase it...at this point, you may just as well read it!

3. Even if you didn't spend any sats on it (diamond hands!!!), you probably at least invested some of your scarce time in downloading this book from some "piracy" site or chat (pirates are badass, and "intellectual property" is a scam, anyway).

4. This book is entertaining, simple, flowing and very easy to read, yet pretty accurate, complete, and compact (remember that Venn thing right?).

5. This book contains quite timeless analyses, yet it fits very nicely in the already pretty large and fast-growing "Svanholm section" you almost certainly already created in your personal library (remember that other Venn thing?).

6. This book is about Bitcoin.

7. This book is not only about Bitcoin: it discusses game theory and praxeology ("Incentives", "Clown World"), cultural history and geopolitics ("Wokeism", "Pendulum"), biology and sociology ("Incentives", "Mind Over Matter"), computer science and (meta?) physics ("We are all Satoshis", "Mind Over Matter"), integrity and honesty ("Slay Your Heroes", "Hill-to-die-on Picking"), and many other topics!

8. This book also discusses never-before-revealed secrets about skateboarders and lightbulbs (I leave it to you to find out where).

9. This book includes many Bitcoin-culture cameos, Easter eggs, and hilarious references (I won't spoil any; have fun finding them).

10. This book showcases the Immortal Wisdom of many important Masters, Philosophers, and Gurus (to mention only a few: Bill Murray and ABBA).

11. This book mentions *me* once. You should always read anything that mentions me (in a positive or neutral way that is). Always.

12. Reading this book is a good way to deepen your understanding of Bitcoin, but also of its reverse (Clown World). Know your enemy.

13. Reading this book is one way to resist low-preference temptations like ingesting seed oils or shilling shitcoins.

14. This book is zero-calorie, carbon-neutral, gluten-free, and vegan (as far as I know).

15. This book can be read by people with blue hair without life-threatening effects.

16. This book can be enjoyed by people who, like me and (seemingly) unlike Knut and Luke, believe in free will, eternal life, the existence of God, and Leibniz's monadology.

17. If you meet Knut and Luke at some Bitcoin conference, you can get this book signed. Maybe you could get away with printing a fake cover and wrapping it around another book, but that seems like a lot of wasted effort and unnecessary risk.

18. Reading this book will either increase your IQ to 120 or reduce it to 80, in both cases bringing you to a safe distance from the midwits that populate Clown World.

19. If they ever end up making a movie out of this book, you will be able to surprise your friends at the premiere by anticipating the plot.

20. This book may finally give you a valid reason to use all those quirky Bitcoin-themed bookmarks you've collected at Bitcoin conferences over the years.

21. If you don't read this book, you may end up having fun staying poor or owning nothing and being happy.

And if, even after all these reasons, you don't believe me about this book or don't get it, I don't have any more time to try to convince you, sorry. But in the other case, enjoy your reading.

Giacomo Zucco

Preface

My journey in Bitcoin started when I moved from Canada to Finland. The call to adventure brought me and my wife halfway across the globe. Amidst the COVID-19 lockdowns and crypto hype of early 2021, I found the Saylor series on the *What Is Money Show*, and I was hooked.

I wanted to contribute to Bitcoin in my own way. I wasn't a developer, so I couldn't contribute directly to Bitcoin itself or to related technical projects, but I was a podcaster (on the supremely useful subject of Norse and Finnish archetypal mythology, but the skills translate). I was drawn to Konsensus Network, the company that translated *The Bitcoin Standard* into Finnish, the obscure little language I was interested in. I responded to a Twitter call for volunteers, and I offered my skills as a podcaster. It was pure synchronicity: they hoped to launch a podcast with one of their authors — the esteemed Knut Svanholm. On August 21st, 2022, The Freedom Footprint Show (FFS for short) was born.

This book is the culmination of the last two years of making this goofy, irreverent, and uncompromising podcast. In 120 episodes and counting at the time of writing, we've conversed with dozens of amazing bitcoiners, sharpening the ideas that made their way into these pages. We acknowledge and thank every one of our guests: this book wouldn't have been made without you.

Although the answer to the question "When did you start writing this book?" is somewhere vaguely between the advent of our separate and melded consciousnesses and the time of publishing, I recall a specific moment in December 2023 when the process really took off. My wife (pregnant with our first child, just at the edge of flying safely) and I visited Knut and his family in Spain, desperate for some sunshine and relaxation in the depths of Finnish winter.

Knut and I went for a long walk together, and on the way, we started talking about his ideas for a new book. He had been complaining that he wanted to write but had severe writer's block for the last few weeks. But now, the juices were starting to flow. We talked about all the big themes we had been discussing lately on the podcast, with the main one being how Bitcoin directly addresses the problems of the fiat world we find ourselves trapped in. Add our focus on the freedom-go-up side of Bitcoin, and the book started to take shape.

The first time the title cropped up was sometime in the preceding few months, on the podcast, naturally. I can't remember the exact episode, but I recall that Knut posited that Bitcoin inverts "Clown World" or is the inverse of Clown World. Of course, "Everything Divided by 21 Million" is further memefied by the equation ∞/21M, and at that moment, a new equation came to mind: "One Divided by Clown World." I recall that we joked about the idea and even suggested that this could be the title of Knut's next book.

Back to our walk in Spain. It was here that we first floated the idea that this could be the theme of the new book: all the ways that Bitcoin inverts Clown World and how, through adopting Bitcoin, you can increase your metaphorical freedom footprint. *Bitcoin: The Inverse of Clown World*, was, if not born, fertilized at that moment.

Still, the book needed to be written first, but in the ensuing weeks, two things happened that kickstarted the whole thing. First, Knut went on a writing spree, producing the bones of at least ten potential chapters. Second, my son arrived into the world five weeks early, at the end of December 2023, which, once he was home safe and healthy, landed me on a period of parental leave unexpectedly early. Between diaper changes and feedings every three hours (during which my wife did the vast majority of the work if I'm completely honest, but I did my best to support her), I had time to talk to Knut about what he had written.

I was as excited as anyone — a new Knut Svanholm book! — and I was honored when he invited me to help him in the editing process. We sat down together and talked about how the chapters would flow, what needed further elaboration, what was repetitive, what might be missing, etc. Our editing sessions became more and more frequent, and the changes to the book became more and more significant. One day, Knut suggested that we were actually writing this together, and invited me to be co-author.

The next time I met Knut in person was during Bitcoin Atlantis on Madeira, an extremely busy but amazingly rewarding weekend on that paradise island. One conversation in the park across the street from the President's mansion led directly to the *Pendulum* chapter. Further discussions led to the last chapter we added - *That Which You Can Do Without* - which I think really ties the book together.

Over the ensuing few months, we held a series of increasingly frequent calls, writing, re-writing, and editing the book into its final form. The natural date to release this book emerged as August 21st, 2024 - Bitcoin Infinity Day, inspired by the Everything Divided by 21 Million meme. When else?

We've both poured our hearts and souls into this book. I'm personally extremely proud of how it turned out. Still, there are some quirks you should be aware of. Due to my later addition as co-author, we have written most addresses to you, the reader, from our joint perspective — "we." However, there are personal anecdotes from Knut that are written from his perspective — "I." It doesn't make sense any other way, and we hope you understand.

This book is intended for bitcoiners. Everything Knut and I do together, to a certain extent, is all about conviction-deepening. We hope that you read this book, consider the ideas presented, and take up the call to increase your freedom footprint in the understanding that, in doing so, you do your part to invert Clown World. We all have our part to play. There is no shortcut. But there is Bitcoin.

Luke de Wolf
July 2024
Helsinki, Finland

Introduction

In the echoing, somewhat banal words of Michael Jackson, "If you wanna make the world a better place, take a look at yourself and then make a change," lies a profound call to action that resonates deeply within the hearts of those of us who dare to dream of a better tomorrow. This timeless nugget of wisdom encapsulates the essence of personal transformation and its ripple effect on the societal fabric surrounding us. A journey of introspection and self-improvement is not just an act of personal fulfillment but a pivotal step towards enacting broader, meaningful change in our interconnected world.

Have you ever found yourself lost in the labyrinth of existential questions? Questions like "Why are we here," "What is the purpose of life," or "How many skateboarders does it take to screw in a lightbulb?" These questions invite us to contemplate our existence and the mysteries surrounding our being. For the curious, the follow-up question "Wait, but why?" soon emerges as a constant companion in our quest for understanding. Our inherent curiosity propels us to challenge the conventional, to look beyond the surface, and to seek truths hidden beneath the veneer of societal norms.

As humans, we constantly strive for coherence and meaning. We have constructed elaborate narratives and frameworks to make sense of our surroundings, and we act like these constructs are immutable truths. Yet, reality is far more fluid. Even when faced with overwhelming evidence, we find it challenging to accept novel ideas. The process of updating conventional wisdom is slow and often comes with a lag. Regardless of what we think about them, new scientific insights and shifts in our technological landscape challenge our perceptions. The dawn of the Internet stands as a testament to this phenomenon.

For example, social media platforms have revolutionized how we perceive our relationships and positions within the global social ecosystem. They act as a double-edged sword, offering us glimpses into the lives of others, for better or worse, revealing facets of character previously concealed in the shadows of our offline interactions. Chances are high that you now view your friends somewhat differently, given the knowledge of what they had for dinner last night. Social media is redefining our concepts of community and belonging, whether we like it or not.

Beyond its capacity to reveal our differences, the Internet, first and foremost, embodies our profound potential for connection. It bridges geographical divides and connects us with individuals and communities that resonate with our deepest values and aspirations. Technologies like social media, video calls, and Bitcoin unveil a horizon of possibilities where the constraints of traditional systems begin to dissolve. The ability to connect with like-minded souls across the globe sends a beacon of hope to those seeking to forge their path, find their tribe, and opt out of systems and structures that no longer serve their highest good. This emerging paradigm champions each individual's right to define their existence, live according to their moral values, and connect with others who share their vision for the world. Opting in is the new opting out.

As we stand on the cusp of a new political reality, the contours of personal freedom and autonomy are becoming increasingly well-defined. The future holds the possibility of an existence where the barriers to living life on one's own terms are ever-diminishing, where the power of voluntarily connected individuals challenges and reshapes the statist quo. Even though the journey toward this new reality is fraught with trade-offs and challenges, it has the potential for unprecedented freedom and philosophical fulfillment.

This book explores the nuances of these trade-offs, examining the essence of freedom and the sacrifices that may be required to achieve it. Hopefully, it will make you challenge some fundamental questions about yourself and reflect on what you would be willing to give up in exchange for a life that genuinely reflects your values and desires. Is this still a Bitcoin book, then? Yes and no, as we shall explore. First and foremost, it is a book about you.

In embarking on this journey through the following pages, we invite you to read with an open heart and a curious mind, reflect on your place in the world, and consider how you can influence it by changing your perspectives. A hill is only worth dying on if it offers a valley to live in.

By the way, it takes three skateboarders to screw in a lightbulb — one to perform the task and two to capture the moment and post it on TikTok.

Incentives

Every action you take, every decision made by governments or corporations, every conflict that arises between nations — all are grounded in the intricate dance of competing incentives and strategies known as game theory. Game theory is a mathematical framework that analyzes strategic interactions between rational decision-makers. It predicts choices and outcomes based on assumptions about preferences and incentives. Understanding game theory and its implications will help you comprehend the world around you and why things are the way they are. Incentives and strategies underpin everything from evolutionary biology to the delicate equilibrium of global politics to the ingenious incentive model underpinning Bitcoin. In other words, game theory permeates every facet of our world.

At its core, game theory is an exploration of strategy. It focuses on how individuals make decisions in situations where the outcome depends not only on their own choices but also on the choices of others. Game theory explains the dynamics of competition and cooperation in many contexts. The approach most likely to win a competition between actors eventually determines reality.

Praxeology, the science of purposeful human action, recognizes two types of competitive behavior — catallactic and biological. Catallactic competition is the non-zero-sum game of free trade, where there are no real losers — only varying degrees of success. In contrast, biological competition is the fang-and-claw, winner-takes-all kind of competition observed in nature.

Catallactic competition refers to the process of rivalry among participants in a market economy. Originating from the Greek word *katallattein*, meaning "to exchange" or "to admit into the community," it was popularized by Austrian School economists like Ludwig von Mises. This form of competition is characterized by voluntary, consensual exchanges and the coordination of individual interests through a free market price mechanism.

In catallactic competition, businesses, consumers, and other market participants compete to achieve their objectives, such as profit maximization for companies and utility maximization for consumers. Prices, which are determined by supply and demand, mediate this competition, guiding resources toward their most valued uses. The free market process is decentralized and information-driven, relying on the spontaneous order that emerges from countless individual decisions rather than on centralized planning. It's a positive-sum game where participants benefit from consensual exchanges.

Conversely, biological competition is a fundamental ecological interaction in which organisms contend for the same limited resources within an environment, such as food, space, or mates. To emphasize, these resources are finite, leading to conflicts where one competitor's success inevitably comes at the expense of another. This process results in natural selection and evolution, as individuals or species more effective at securing resources are more likely to survive and reproduce.

While the distinction between catallactics and biology is helpful for rational thought processes and deductive reasoning, purely biological or purely catallactic interactions in human societies are rare, to say the least. In the so-called free market economies of the world, inflation, taxes, and market interventions are everywhere. Most, if not all, of these phenomena are not entirely consensual and thus not purely catallactic. If you don't pay your taxes, men with guns will eventually knock on your door and remove your freedoms by force. Such an action is a display of biological competition, not catallactics.

Just as biological competition can be observed within praxeology, market-like catallactic competition appears in nature, too. Fang-and-claw is by no means the only method of resolving conflict over scarce resources available to animals and plants. A single ant cannot survive for very long without the intricacies of the barter economy of the ant hill. Ants trade pheromones, sticks, mud, and other resources, without which their foresty fortresses and clay castles couldn't exist.

Another example is the symbiotic relationship between bees and flowers. Flowers provide nectar to bees, while bees facilitate pollination for flowers. Despite the potential for either party to "cheat" — bees could take nectar without pollinating, or flowers could offer no nectar — the mutually beneficial strategy of cooperation prevails. So, what can game theory tell us about how collaboration and catallactics first emerged in nature? Let's find out, shall we?

The Prisoner's Dilemma is a specific scenario in game theory that illustrates why two rational individuals might not cooperate, even if it appears that it is in their best interest to do so. Imagine two prisoners are suspected of committing a crime jointly but interrogated separately. Each prisoner is given the choice to betray the other by testifying against them (defect) or to band together by remaining silent (cooperate). Their prison sentences will be based on how they choose to act. If both defect, they receive moderate sentences, but if one defects and the other remains silent, the betrayer is freed, while the silent one receives a harsh sentence. If both remain silent, they get minor sentences. This simple dilemma sets out the conflict between individual self-interest and mutual benefit, often leading to suboptimal outcomes for both parties.

For example, Craig is a snake-oil salesman, and his uncle Calvin sometimes helps him scam people. One day, Agent Threeletter arrests them and starts interrogating the duo. Agent Threeletter knows he hasn't enough evidence to convict Craig and Calvin for a pyramid scheme unless one turns on the other. Therefore, he decides to separate the two and offers each the same deal: if one rats out the other, the rat will be freed immediately while the other faces twenty years of soap-picking in the showers of San Quentin. If they both blame each other, they will both receive a rather lengthy ten years in the slammer. However, if they refrain from playing the blame game altogether, Craig and Calvin will be charged with a minor offense and receive a paltry five years in a nice Norwegian daycare center. Faced with these options, Craig and Calvin must decide independently whether to betray the other or remain silent, each without knowing what the other will choose. (In this particular case, though, the perpetrators both died from AIDS before the trial had even begun, and Agent Threeletter retired early to play Bloons every day for the rest of his life.)

What can we learn? If a Prisoner's Dilemma type scenario happens only once, the optimal strategy is to betray the other prisoner. A prisoner who does so faces either a moderate sentence or is set free. On the other hand, a prisoner who remains silent (cooperates) is either given a harsh or a minor sentence. Overall, the former option seems better than the latter — especially since you cannot know what your opponent will do. The prisoners both have the incentive to betray one another. But what if the same game is played over and over again? How would that change the game's dynamics, and what would be the best strategy in the long run?

With its options to cooperate or defect, the Prisoner's Dilemma mirrors real-world conflicts and natural phenomena, illustrating how repeated interactions impact strategic choices. A 1980 computer tournament organized by political scientist Robert Axelrod brought new insights into the Dilemma by letting players play it repeatedly using various strategies. As it turns out, when the game is played in perpetuity (or for some unknown number of times), the winning tactic is a strategy called "Tit for Tat."

A player using "Tit for Tat" chooses to cooperate by default and only defects as a direct response to the opponent defecting first, resulting in an appropriate eye-for-an-eye moral response. After retaliating against the opponent's defection, the "Tit for Tat" player then switches back to their original cooperation strategy, giving their opponent the benefit of the doubt. Defection only becomes an option should the other player choose to defect again.

The tactic embodies simplicity and reciprocity and relates to cooperation and retaliation in politics, international relations, and even evolutionary biology. Axelrod's findings emphasized the importance of being friendly and forgiving, but also appropriately retaliatory. In Theodor Roosevelt's words, "Speak softly and carry a big stick." These principles underscore the complex dynamics of cooperation and conflict resolution, regardless of whether we're discussing ant hills or nuclear warhead management. Ultimately, this evolution of collaboration, even among self-centered individuals, highlights that it is in one's best long-term interest to be honest rather than to try to deceive whichever opponent you happen to face.

The final scene in Christopher Nolan's *The Dark Knight* depicts our innate proclivity for non-aggression. As the scene unfolds, the Joker has trapped two distinct segments of Gotham's population on two ferries. One ferry is full of innocent people, and the other carries the city's worst criminals. The Joker then tells them he intends to blow up both ferries at midnight unless one ferry chooses to blow up the other first. Both ferries are given a detonator device that the Joker claims will blow up the other ferry. The scene ends with the criminals throwing the detonator out a window, and although the civilians vote to blow up the criminals, when push comes to shove, the ferry captain can't bring himself to pull the trigger.

Batman stories are (allegedly) fictional, but there are many real-world examples where people abstain from casting the first stone. The rationale for this behavior can be derived from the simple logic of which personality traits provided an evolutionary advantage throughout the history of life on this planet. No species would have gotten very far without cooperation.

Speaking of bats, the mutual nurturing behavior of vampire bats highlights the "Tit-for-Tat" tactic in nature. These bats often share blood meals with fellow hungry bats because they know the favor will be returned in the future. Reciprocal altruism ensures that bats who share their resources will receive help when needed, encouraging cooperation and social cohesion within the group.

The BitTorrent network, a peer-to-peer file-sharing protocol, is an example of "Tit-for-Tat" from the internet. The network's users enhance their download speeds by employing a cooperation/defection "Tit-for-Tat" strategy, which is necessary since BitTorrent peers have a finite number of upload slots to share with others. When a peer's upload bandwidth reaches its limit, it adopts "Tit-for-Tat" to prioritize cooperative peers — those who exchange upload bandwidth for download bandwidth. If a peer does not reciprocate by uploading, the BitTorrent software restricts its connection until the uncooperative peer begins uploading again.

Axelrod's Prisoner's Dilemma tournament underscores a fundamental truth: the balance between self-interest and cooperative behavior is crucial in the game of life, where decisions shape futures. This balance, encoded in our very nature, demonstrates the impact of strategic choices on our individual and collective destinies. Empirical evidence suggests that, more often than not, the best long-term strategy is to be cooperative.

As we navigate life's complex web of interactions, the wisdom from game theory — to be kind, forgiving, firm in response, and transparent — guides us toward a more harmonious coexistence. We are wired to optimize individual outcomes and, in doing so, contribute to a more cooperative and peaceful world. Is there a more comforting thought than knowing that being kind and just is how you beat the game of evolution?

Also embedded in the web of interactions is the concept that the more willing you are to delay gratification, the more likely you are to play the game correctly, which benefits everyone. In the end, consensual cooperation not only prevails but saves us all. All that's required for this timeline to play out is kindness and appropriate responses to injustices. The former is easy, but the latter can be tricky. Appropriate responses require you to know your enemy. Unfortunately, many bad actors are good at hiding their true intentions and have considerable political power...

Our brains are hardwired to react more strongly to threats and bad news than to positive information. A newspaper with headlines like "Everyone lives longer now!" or "Crime rates are dropping!" wouldn't sell many copies. Fear sells, which is something both journalists and politicians are aware of. This is nothing new, of course, and the way human hierarchical power structures are set up is largely a product of our leaders' ability to play on these fears and gain popular support by exaggerating both the alleged problems and the efficiency of their supposed solutions. In many (if not most) cases, our societies would have been better off not caring so much.

Democratic systems, for example, are not as consensual as advertised. Modern nation-states depend on mandatory public schooling, taxation, and central banking. These systems have only been around for a few hundred years, yet they pervade our societies so intensely it's as if we've never been without them. Citizens can vote for political parties that promise to lower one tax or scrap another, but inflation ensures that taxes always trend upward. Furthermore, a public institution behaves like any other type of tumor — it grows and grows, and the only way to stop the process is to remove it altogether.

Reconfiguring society presents a Sisyphean task. Public schooling and state-subsidized media feed the democracy narrative, and most people think societal problems are most efficiently solved via the ballot box. Politicians faced with re-election can't resist promising fancy goodies to potential voters, and someone has to pay eventually. If it's not through taxes, it's through inflationary currency enabled by central banks, and there is no way to entirely opt out of the fiat system as long as governments require taxes paid in their national currencies. The most insidious thing is that inflation is a sneakily gradual process. The frog in the boiling pot doesn't jump out since he doesn't realize he's being cooked alive. He will keep voting for more heat.

The long arm of the law allows the eager fingers of the taxman and the central banker to pickpocket you without you even noticing the hidden threat of violence backing up these actions. Refuse to pay, and you'll soon find out what this means. You've been lulled into thinking that *some* non-consensual interactions are morally okay through decades of programming by public schooling and mainstream media outlets financed and subsidized by the pickpockets themselves. But taxes, and especially inflation, are neither natural nor moral phenomena. Like everything else in society, they are the products of deliberate decisions.

If the game you're playing is rigged such that you cannot retaliate appropriately when you're being deceived, your only option is to find a better game. A game where the cost of deceit dwarves the potential temporary gain to such an extent that cheating becomes a pointless endeavor. In our day and age, there is only one such game in town — Bitcoin. Bitcoin provides each and every one of us with a crucial choice — the choice to opt out of unfair games. To understand Bitcoin properly, specifically what problem it solves, we must first understand human action.

Like mathematics and game theory, the science of human action is not empirical. Therefore, the underlying axioms praxeology is built upon cannot be refuted without running into logical contradictions. For example, the statement "Every voluntary exchange is perceived as beneficial by both parties involved, lest the exchange will not happen" cannot be refuted without inconsistencies. If either party didn't find it beneficial, the exchange could still happen, but it wouldn't be voluntary.

By the same token, the statements, "An increase in the supply of a currency higher than the increase in the corresponding goods and services you can buy for that currency, can never lead to lower prices," or indeed, "A coercive exchange may be of short-term benefit to the coercer, but never to the coerced," are also logically consistent and thus irrefutable.

These statements don't have to be shown to be accurate by observation but are irrefutable logical conclusions. As Voltaire bemoaned, common sense is not very common. Most people view threats, deceit, and coercion as natural phenomena — something we all just have to accept and live with. Democracy is still the least worst form of governance there is, right? Right?!? Few understand the implications of such acceptance, and even fewer know that alternative modi operandi exist.

It's also important to note that "voluntary" is not the same as "consensual." For example, a person being robbed might voluntarily give up his Rolex watch in exchange for his life without necessarily consenting to the interaction. The same is true for most tax-payers — taxes are, for the most part, voluntarily paid because the tax-payer finds paying them a better option than jail. This does not make them consensual. In fact, the government calling you a tax-payer is a bit like a rapist calling his victim his girlfriend.

Many a word has been written about the benefits of a free market system, the history of money, and the horrors of totalitarianism. However, most people are still clueless about how horrendous the butterfly effects can be following even the slightest politicization of the free market process. In a world where correct pronoun assignments, teenaged weather activists, the big game last night, Taylor Swift's latest boyfriend, and a mostly harmless flu are headline news, it's easy to see that some force is trying to avert our eyes from the men behind the curtain. But what force put these men behind said curtain in the first place, and what can be done to reverse the process?

The two towering figures of the Austrian School of Economics, Ludwig von Mises and Murray Rothbard, described the state's rapacious nature similarly to the examples above, yet they were critical of the applicability and relevance of game theory to economics. They both argued that praxeology's methodological and philosophical foundations differ from those underpinning game theory.

Though not extensively discussing game theory directly in his works, Mises laid the framework of praxeology, which emphasizes individual decision-making based on subjective values and preferences. From a Misesian perspective, economics should focus on understanding individuals' purposeful actions rather than mathematical models or predictive systems, like those often employed in game theory. Mises critiqued game theory for its reliance on mathematical abstraction and for its assumptions of fixed preferences and information symmetry among participants. He argued that such models can only partially capture human action's dynamic and subjective nature, which is crucial to economic analysis.

Rothbard offered even more direct critiques of game theory. Acknowledging the intellectual allure of game theory, Rothbard criticized its practical utility in economic analysis. Given game theory's focus on static equilibria and defined payoff matrices, Rothbard was particularly skeptical of its capacity to provide meaningful insights into market processes and the actions of entrepreneurs.

One should, of course, refrain from drawing unfounded conclusions about economics and human choices. The Austrian Economists were right to leave mathematics out of economics because subjective value judgments can not be quantified. If, however, we maintain separation between these two sciences and admit that they describe vastly different things, they can provide us with better "truth goggles" through which to view the world.

So, back to Axelrod! What a lovely name for a mathematician, don't you think? His findings did not come from a priori deductive reasoning but from simply testing various strategies against one another and observing the results. To what extent repeated, relatively simple game theoretical games accurately represent real-world events is thus impossible to know. Empiricism does not allow for irrefutable claims like a priori deductive reasoning does. What it can do, though, is provide tools to make your view of history increasingly accurate.

It's important not to throw out the baby with the bathwater when it comes to empiricism. One of humanity's best ideas, the scientific method arguably propelled our species forward more during the Enlightenment than any preceding era.

Game theory and praxeology are both about understanding incentives and their role in our interactions, but the things they describe and how they describe them differ vastly. Methodologically, they are similar, as both rely on axiomatic logical deduction. Game theory studies mathematical models of strategic interactions among rational agents, while praxeology studies purposeful action per se. A deeper understanding of both subjects can inject a healthy dose of optimism into an otherwise bleak world.

At the end of the day, our actions dictate our future. Game theory can tell us the most probable outcome of a particular strategy, but without our individual, deliberate actions, there can be no strategy at all. You decide how you want to play whatever game you choose to participate in. You decide when to give the benefit of the doubt and when to retaliate. No one can decide these things but you. What reality you end up in depends on your choices, regardless of when or where you happened to be born. Accepting this is a good starting point in the perpetual quest for freedom, which we all have to partake in sooner or later, whether we know it or not.

Wokeism

In the cloak-and-dagger world of Cold War espionage, one man's crisis of conscience proved more potent than the propaganda machine he once served. Yuri Bezmenov, born in 1939 in the Soviet Moscow suburb of Mytishchi, had been trained as a master of deception by the notorious KGB. After cutting his teeth spreading disinformation with the press arm of the Soviet Army, Bezmenov went to work for the Novosti Press Agency in 1963, all while moonlighting as an informant for the KGB itself. But after over a decade of disseminating lies on an industrial scale, Bezmenov made the ultimate defection — abandoning the rotten core of the Soviet system he could no longer tolerate. His daring escape to the West in 1970 put his life in the crosshairs, leading him to assume a new identity as Tomas David Schuman in Canada. Yet this was only the beginning of the high-stakes journey for the disillusioned agent, determined to expose the sinister machinery of subversion where he had once thrived.

In the West, Bezmenov became known for his lectures and interviews about his KGB experiences, in which he warned about Soviet espionage tactics. He focused on the concept of ideological subversion, a process he described as a slow method of brainwashing or psychological warfare aimed at changing the perception and behavior of entire societies. He emphasized that this subversion was more dangerous than conventional espionage because it sought to destabilize and demoralize nations from within. The popular image of intelligence work, fueled by Hollywood and mainstream media, distorts the reality of Cold War tactics. According to Bezmenov, the KGB dedicated only about a sixth of its budget to actual espionage. The bulk, a staggering 85%, was spent on a more insidious objective — catalyzing a gradual ideological shift in the West. Rather than target abrupt, overnight impact, the KGB's influence operation was meticulously crafted to work gradually and persistently, steadily reshaping mindsets and beliefs.

Bezmenov divides the process of Soviet-style ideological subversion into four stages:

Demoralization. This initial and most protracted phase, spanning up to 20 years, involves gradually undermining a nation's values and beliefs. The goal is to alter the perceptions of an entire generation. In the context of the United States, this meant exposure to Marxist-Leninist ideology, subtly injected into the education system and cultural discourse, as happened during the Cold War.

Destabilization. Rather than altering beliefs, this stage focuses on destabilizing the targeted nation's economy, foreign relations, and defense systems — a disruption to the fundamental structures that keep a society functioning properly.

Crisis. A potentially rapid phase (often as brief as six weeks) is marked by significant upheaval or unrest, ultimately leading to radical changes in the targeted nation's power structure and economy.

Normalization. The ultimate objective, this stage cynically rebrands the subversive elements' consolidation of power as the "new normal," ushering in a new statist quo.

The first phase, Demoralization, is particularly significant. Its effects are long-lasting and, in many cases, irreversible. It renders a population unable to discern factual information or to make rational decisions in their best interests. The indoctrination infiltrates so profoundly that even in the presence of overwhelming evidence against their beliefs, the demoralized individuals refuse to acknowledge obvious truths about their reality. Does this sound familiar, dear reader?

Bezmenov warned that the process of Demoralization in the United States had not only been completed but even exceeded expectations. Even if efforts to reverse the trend were initiated, it would take another 15 to 20 years to undo the damage. Although Bezmenov's message is from the 80s, ideological subversion is still a clear and present danger. Today, with success assured, it operates not in the shadows but in plain sight, manipulating perceptions and altering the fabric of society.

Even though the outward-facing KGB disappeared alongside the rest of the Soviet Union in the early 90s, the propagandistic modus operandi of this charming organization seems almost embedded in the DNA of all collectivist ideologues. The KGB was not the first nor will it be the last collectivist institution to harness the power of indoctrination. In a similar fashion to how pedophiles are drawn to careers involving child care, collectivists can be found all over mass media outlets and universities. When polls about political affiliations are conducted among journalists, the results tilt overwhelmingly to the left. The same is true for academia. These fields often self-select for people who believe societal problems can and ought to be solved by rallying the masses to advance specific causes. Social engineering ideology speaks to the inherent narcissism of the highly educated intellectual: "That wasn't real communism, but I know how to do it the right way."

Looking at essential human personality traits, it's easy to see why shifts toward collectivization have happened frequently throughout history. Collectivists tend to be more agreeable than individualists, which is unsurprising given the category labels. Agreeableness is the "why can't we all just get along" personality trait. If you regard group agreement as inherently valuable, you're more likely to sacrifice other things to achieve it. If honesty is to be sacrificed, agreement must come at the truth's expense.

The belief that the world is divided strictly between the mega-rich and the super-poor is a misconception. Most people fall into a middle-income category, but mainstream media and politicians trying to win votes from people's emotional responses reinforce the skewed perception of global poverty. Countless human development metrics show significant improvement over time, challenging the bleak outlook portrayed by the media. Today, when the global free market has made everything so cheap that extreme poverty is approximately just a third of what it was at the beginning of the millennium, collectivists have had to come up with new ways of framing the class war. What used to be a struggle between the proletariat and the bourgeoisie has now transformed into an orchestrated battle between certain minority groups and straight, white, middle-aged men.

The multifarious Marxist infiltration of academia and mass media is easy to spot. Woke ideology is everywhere. When actual Marxist infiltration tactics mix with the tendency of the media and academia to attract self-righteous collectivists, everything falls apart. The more the blue-haired, non-cis-gendered revolutionaries climb the institutional ladders, the more dysfunctional these institutions become. Wokeism abounds in social and political activism, especially around social justice, race, gender, and environmentalism, which is why you hear so much about these superficial topics and so little about actual problems.

One example of Marxist infiltration is the movement in educational institutions to "decolonize" the curriculum. Decolonization involves reevaluating and changing the content of courses to reduce the historical role of Western civilization in favor of an allegedly more inclusive, global perspective — one that emphasizes the contributions and cultures of previously marginalized societies. While the stated intention of this initiative is to create a more balanced and inclusive educational environment, it more often than not downplays important historical events and achievements, particularly those involving white men on the "winning" side. Funnily enough (or perhaps strategically), the role of the money printer in shaping society hardly ever makes it into the curriculum, decolonized or otherwise.

Moreover, governments and institutions in some Western countries have introduced policies to use "gender-neutral" language in official documents and communications. For example, to be more inclusive of non-binary and transgender individuals, certain jurisdictions have adopted the use of "they/them" pronouns or gender-neutral titles like "Mx." Some countries have outright criminalized the act of "misgendering" people.

Similarly, universities and related institutions across the Western world have created "safe spaces" and implemented trigger warnings to "protect" students from potentially distressing content or discussions. The intention is to promote an environment where all students feel safe and supported, particularly those from "marginalized" groups. However, these practices have the exact opposite effect of their stated intention, resulting in an adversarial environment where the victimhood hierarchy matters more than intellectual achievement. When debate is stifled, dogma replaces curiosity. Ideas only thrive when questioned.

We hardly even need to mention the destructiveness of climate alarmism. Long-term, sustainable thinking is being sacrificed on the altar of political cosmetics on an almost daily basis. Part of the climate mob "wants you to panic." Panicking is the opposite of long-term planning and is not "sustainable" in any way, shape, or form. The seriousness of the issue can be debated, but debate is only possible if both parties are willing to listen.

The prevailing "power analysis" mindset of the woke world is a simplistic concept that has gained traction precisely because it requires minimal intellectual effort. "Power analysis" operates on a simple premise: based solely on gut feeling, the group that seemingly deserves the most sympathy is granted priority in claiming victimhood. The Marxists of the 21st century are no longer upset about group wealth inequalities but are more concerned with which group to signal that they pity the most.

"Power analysis" leads to skewed perspectives where, for example, it's socially acceptable for women to express disdain towards men but not the reverse. Yet, women are not allowed to object to the penis-haver in their dressing room. It's also only acceptable for individuals to express prejudice based on body size in a one-sided manner — no one's upset about "skinny-shaming." Similarly, derogatory terms aimed at immigrants are considered more offensive than those aimed at natives.

It all leads to the Oppression Olympics, where you win by defending the most marginalized group you can come up with. Whether your marginalized group is throwing people of another marginalized group off rooftops doesn't matter, so long as the former is perceived to be more oppressed than the latter. Where a particular group sits on the victimhood scale whimsically changes over time, but consistency is of little concern to people playing this game. They only care about signaling; the loudest voice usually gets the attention they so desperately crave. Clown World™ is in full swing.

Although it's hard for most to see, fractional reserve banking is the main engine that drives the entire circus caravan. Monetary expansion triggers the Cantillon Effect, which funnels wealth from those furthest away from the money printer to those closest to it — the most politically connected. When left to function on its own, the free market rewards productivity and efficiency while punishing laziness and inadequate risk management. The more politicized the free market process grows, the more hampered the effects of this natural phenomenon become. The not-so-free market with inflationary money and high taxes rewards political correctness rather than value creation.

Once on the slippery slope of collectivist takeover, societies soon start showing significant signs of decay. One prominent indication is how obedience becomes a virtue, regardless of whether the law being obeyed is ethically sound. During the latter stages of the horrendous lockdowns during the COVID-19 pandemic, local rules changed frequently, and knowing which guideline-de-jour to follow at the moment became a marker of how good of a citizen you were. Mass psychosis is a genuine phenomenon, and the human race can be pretty scary whenever it occurs. History is littered with examples, from Nazi Germany to Mao's China, to the USSR, to North Korea. They all had one thing in common: they valued the collective above the individual.

One cannot escape or stop collectivism by being a collectivist oneself. Only when you come to this realization do you stand a chance of escaping the Matrix and bypassing Clown World altogether. The only way to avoid the perils of collectivism is to carve your own path, to be an individualist first and foremost, and to think for yourself. This is a continuous battle that never ends. As Ronald Reagan said:

> "Freedom is never more than one generation away from extinction. We didn't pass it to our children in the bloodstream. It must be fought for, protected, and handed on for them to do the same, or one day, we will spend our sunset years telling our children and our children's children what it was once like in the United States, where men were free."

Clownish political ideas have existed for as long as politics itself. They come in many ways, shapes, and forms, and it can be hard to see their ridiculousness when living among them. There are methods for detecting clownishness, though — one of the most effective is first-principles rational thinking. From a first-principles perspective, there can only be one logically consistent human right: the right to be left alone.

The right to be left alone is the only human right that doesn't require violating someone else's rights. It is the fundamental moral and ethical underpinning of the libertarian idea of the non-aggression principle, which, in turn, is the foundation of absolute property rights. No country on Earth currently adheres to these principles. The notion of a government and a monopoly on violence inherently contradicts the non-aggression principle.

It doesn't matter who the enforcing group is — governments, religious cohorts, drug cartels, football hooligans, mafiosos — if you're being punished for a victimless crime, you are the victim. From a strict consensualist, non-aggressive ethical perspective, a crime always involves violating property rights; otherwise, it's not a crime.

If aliens ever landed on Earth, they would find most human activities confusing, to say the least. It is likely that aliens also construct homes and reproduce, but whether they baptize their kids, cheer for sports teams, or organize pride festivities is questionable. If they do, they probably do so peacefully, without trying to enforce their hobbies onto others. If the aliens are technologically sophisticated enough for interstellar travel, they must have dropped crusades, hooliganism, and the persecution of pronoun misusers long ago. Unfounded violence is never the civilized solution to any problem.

Silence, contrary to popular belief, is not violence. Silencing others by force is. Unless you're doing it on your property, where you set the rules. This is just one of the reasons why property rights are more important than freedom of speech laws. If you don't wish to be robbed of your possessions, you have to accept that it's not morally okay for you to demand that others be robbed of theirs. Since every country on Earth robs its citizens to some extent, this live-and-let-live type of lifestyle is only possible through barter or Bitcoin. Barter requires a mutual coincidence of wants and has no practical usefulness in the modern world. Bitcoin, on the other hand, is an agreement on a fixed set of rules for peaceful interactions between people, not a top-down system you can't opt out of.

When money is nothing but information, confiscating it becomes much more challenging. It is impossible to know how much Bitcoin another person owns since the coins are literally in their owners' heads. In the long term, this changes everything because it reduces the profitability of violent behavior. Stealing information from someone's memory is inherently more complex than confiscating their physical possessions. Information, especially when stored in someone's head, is intangible and can only be physically seized with the individual's cooperation or using coercive techniques that still do not guarantee success. In contrast, physical possessions are tangible and much more easily confiscated. For both the taxman and the highway robber, Bitcoin poses a threat to their livelihoods.

Moreover, information in a person's memory is not directly accessible to others without the individual revealing it willingly. Even then, the accuracy of the retrieved information is hard to verify. If a perpetrator manages to force a bitcoiner to give up his Bitcoin, there is no way of knowing if the stolen amount was all there was. It is possible to keep more than one secret. Once shared or extracted, information can be replicated endlessly without degrading the original "copy" in someone's memory. None of this is true for physical possessions.

In contexts where coordination or conflict involves securing information rather than physical assets, the usefulness of violence diminishes due to the intrinsic differences in how information and physical possessions are controlled and protected. Acquisition strategies change when the asset resides in someone's memory — traditional leverage methods become less effective. Therefore, the incentives for everyone shift towards voluntarism — offering something in return, in other words. As a result, consensual free market exchanges become more profitable than violent confiscations, even for the taxman and the highway robber.

In a hyperbitcoinized world (where information is more valuable than physical assets) reliability, loyalty, and honesty become commodities in their own right. Your reputation becomes your most valuable asset next to your Bitcoin stack. We have merely scratched the surface of how revolutionary and transformative the discovery of Bitcoin really was.

It can be hard to see the violence inherent in every government policy, but at the end of the day, not obeying the law inevitably leads to men with guns taking your freedoms away. Extrapolate all the way to the end, and you'll realize that even not putting tampons in your men's room can lead to your losing a part of your life, liberty, and/or property. Every modest fine for a victimless crime is a property violation. In reality, a "microaggression" is not what the woke mob thinks it is. Offending someone by using the wrong pronoun may sound aggressive, but there's no actual violence involved. Woke policies and regulations, on the other hand, are all actually aggressive since they're ultimately enforced by men with guns. A term like "macroaggression" is more appropriate — to describe *their* actions.

Most people are clueless about how free they could be if they viewed the world differently and used the right tools. The majority of all populations in all countries are lulled and brainwashed into believing that some people have the right to make decisions for others. The only thing making this intersubjective delusion somewhat true is the monopoly on violence that all governments possess within their borders. The battle against collective subversion cannot be won with weapons but with the dissemination of information, the cultivation of critical thinking, and an unwavering commitment to first-principles thinking.

Clown World

Ask anyone what the most pressing political issue in the world is today, and you'll get a wildly different answer depending on who you ask. Climate change, nuclear threats, misinformation, censorship, corporate greed - the responses will run the gamut. But drill down, and you'll find a common thread underlying these problems, something most people miss entirely: the urge for there to be a free lunch. From individuals to nations, we share an innate desire to reap rewards without paying the costs. Until we shed this delusion and accept that every action has consequences, we'll remain trapped in a perpetual cycle of new crises spawning from the attempts to solve old ones.

Robert Heinlein's famous adage, "There is no such thing as a free lunch," encapsulates a fundamental economic principle that nothing is ever given away for free without a cost somewhere to someone. The phrase highlights that even if something appears to be free, costs are always involved, though they might be hidden or distributed in ways that are not immediately apparent. The concept is grounded in the understanding that resources are limited, and any goods or services provided "for free" must still be produced and delivered. The stereotypical "free lunch" is that you'll have your meal paid for, but only if you agree to watch this short sales presentation or sign up for the "free" first week of this fantastic subscription.

Chances are high that if you're reading this, you live in what people commonly refer to as a "liberal democracy." Most people believe that liberal democracies spring from the ideas of liberalism and the will of the people. But is there any empirical evidence to support these claims? Furthermore, what do we mean by "democracy," and who are we referring to when we talk about "the will of the people?"

When was the last time you heard anyone say, "Oh, how I'd love to move to a country with a more inflationary currency where I can pay higher taxes!" or "What I'd really like is to get less for more!"? If given a choice, most people would like to pay lower taxes. Some think others should pay more taxes, but for some reason, they never believe *they* should. Still, almost everyone fails to see the inherent flaws in this argument. All liberal democracies trend toward higher tax burdens and more inflation if you zoom out a few decades. Political scientists blame this phenomenon on several factors, but the underlying cause is often overlooked.

Let's explore some basic praxeological facts. Before a 100% consensual and voluntary transaction between two people occurs, both parties must necessarily value whatever the other party offers more than whatever they are willing to exchange for it. If this isn't the case, the trade won't happen. Conversely, if a transaction is non-consensual and involuntary, the trade MUST occur at the expense of the party being forced to give something up. In other words, consensual transactions are a net benefit to all participants, while non-consensual ones only benefit one party and punish the other. These statements are all true a priori, meaning empirical observations cannot confirm nor deny their validity.

It is also important to stress that all human interactions are transactions. If two people merely talk, they exchange value with each other (and if governments could tax conversations, they certainly would). Conversants would remain silent if they didn't believe that allocating bodily energy to their vocal cords and producing sounds to form words for the other person to hear was worth it. Everything has a tradeoff, and everything is a trade. You even trade with *yourself* if you forgo immediate pleasure for consumption on a rainy day!

If all transactions were utterly devoid of interventionism and coercion, everyone would stand to gain something from every interaction with another human being. Therefore, "society" should, above all else, strive to remove as many non-consensual interactions between people as possible. So why isn't this the primary concern of all governments? Because governments aren't society! Society is you and me. Once you understand what this implies, you'll begin seeing the world through a different lens.

Theoretically, democratic elections should mitigate the risk of taxes running amok. If the taxes become too burdensome for people, they will vote for parties that want to decrease them, right? So why doesn't this ever happen? Why are virtually all democratic governments growing in size and intrusiveness? To understand this question, we must first understand how incentives dictate people's lives.

Democracy, often hailed as the epitome of fair governance, is a system where the majority's decision through free and fair elections supposedly determines the political direction of the jurisdiction. Despite their widespread adoption and alleged inherent value in promoting freedom and equality, democratic systems are fundamentally flawed for several reasons:

One of the more significant criticisms of democracy is the "tyranny of the majority." This tyranny occurs when the majority's interests consistently prevail at the expense of minority rights and interests. The majority often enforce policies that are detrimental to minority groups and individuals, leading to social divisions and injustice. Four people making a four-out-of-five majority decision to beat up and steal from the fifth person is not particularly ethical.

Moreover, elected officials often prioritize policies with immediate benefits to secure re-election, neglecting long-term needs and sustainability. This short-term focus leads to inadequate investment and resource misallocation. Critical societal functions like infrastructure, education, and environmental protection require long-term planning and commitment. Democracies seldom hold space for long-term projects since the next election is always around the corner. Just look at the myopic shutdowns of several nuclear reactors in Europe, where appeasing confused climate alarmists resulted in the opposite effects of what those alarmists so stridently advocated for. Another example would be the Keystone XL pipeline project in Alberta, Canada, which was initiated, canceled, reinstated, and then canceled again because of US election outcomes ping-ponging between Team Blue and Team Red. Democracies struggle to make and implement tough decisions that are unpopular in the short term but beneficial in the long run. More often than not, the need for consensus or the fear of losing electoral support leads to gridlock or the avoidance of necessary reforms.

Functioning democracies rely on an informed and engaged electorate. In other words — there are no functioning democracies. In most countries, citizens have one vote each, regardless of how informed they are about anything. Most voters lack sufficient knowledge to make informed decisions about *almost anything*, leading to choices based on superficial criteria or even blatant misinformation. Equality is, in many ways, the opposite of quality.

Democracies are also inherently susceptible to populism and demagoguery, where leaders gain support by appealing to popular desires and prejudices rather than using rational arguments. In fact, an election is nothing but a popularity contest — populists always win, even if they claim to be nothing of the kind. Democratically elected leaders seldom have the best qualifications or intentions for the country's governance because such things have virtually nothing to do with the election process.

Furthermore, those with substantial financial resources significantly influence the democratic process. Campaign financing, lobbying, and political advertising sway public opinion and policy decisions, often prioritizing corporate interests and pet projects over people's actual needs.

Voters generally vote for parties willing to spend government funds on them. Whether this is through subsidizing the sector they work in or straight-up government funding doesn't matter. The average voter is not very likely to cast a vote that bites the hand that feeds him. In the so-called public sector, no one wants a smaller government. Furthermore, if you're unemployed and in a social welfare program, you're even more unlikely to vote for parties that would unplug your financial life support. The larger the government grows, the more people become dependent on it, and the less likely they are to reduce its size via the ballot box.

Politicians have lives outside of politics, too. Most of them have families, and they all have dreams and personal goals. They might have entered politics because of their passion for a specific cause at a young age, but that initial spark tends to fade as they grow older. As they mature, politicians start caring more for their families and less about what got them into politics in the first place. To rise within the party and become a successful politician, you must tuck away your strong personal opinions and align with party groupthink.

The parties themselves are also under the influence of incentives. When a political party is founded, it's usually because impassioned founding members bond over a set of core principles. However, as the party grows, it becomes challenging to stick to the genesis principles as more and more party members' individual opinions must be blended into the movement. The party is a democracy in itself and comes with the same set of challenges all democracies do.

If a political party is going to win an election or at least get as many votes as possible, it must throw its principles out the window. The most successful parties shape their campaigns based on whatever they think the majority thinks. Elections are not about which party best represents the most distinct political philosophy. Nor is it about whoever best explains why their ideology is better than everyone else's. The winning party is the one that molds its message around whatever direction the electoral school of fish is swimming in right around election day. All political parties are, therefore, inherently populist — all of them. A democratic election is nothing but a popularity contest.

For a political party to stay in power, it must uphold the facade of progress. The most efficient way to do so is to take on more national debt and spend frivolously on grandiose structures and reforms no one asked for. Nations rarely intend to repay their mounting debt; rather, they accumulate more to keep pace with their rivals. A government's default option to reduce this burden is to embark on the economically destructive path of printing more fiat currency. The temptation to overspend while deferring costs proves irresistible. Remember, the only way a government can extract value from its subjects is to take it by force.

Governments invoke three ways to take your stuff against your will. The first and most obvious way is to tax you, and governments don't want it to be too evident that taking your stuff is what they're doing. Therefore, they tend to tax things you are less likely to notice. Corporate taxes, import tariffs, sales taxes, and other taxes ultimately punish *you*, the consumer. Another thing governments do to keep up the facade that taxes are fair and legitimate is to make people in the public sector pay them, too. Why? Taxes pay public sector employees, so why go through the bothersome process of paying them too much and making them pay back parts of their salaries? The only reason for this is to deceive you into thinking that the public sector is just as much a part of the nation's economy as the private one. It isn't.

The second thing governments can do to blacken the red figures on their balance sheets is to cut spending. However, doing so is also a form of covert theft since you, the taxpayer, are now deprived of the service you didn't ask for but already paid for.

A third method by which governments can indirectly appropriate wealth from their citizens is by expanding the country's money supply. Monetary inflation diminishes the value of the national currency, effectively reducing the actual cost of the national debt. This process tends to redistribute wealth from those without assets to those who hold them, with the government itself often being the principal owner of said assets within its borders.

Cutting spending is the only one of these three measures that can be considered semi-consensual. But at its core, even that is more akin to theft than cooperation. "Nothing in this world is certain, except death and taxes," the saying goes, and the taxman has been around for at least as long as governments have. The phenomenon of taxes is only justified in the eyes of the taxpayers because they wish for there to be a shortcut to societal progress — a free lunch. But there is no such thing. Nor is there such a thing as a brunch or a second breakfast. It doesn't matter what you call the meal — you can only break your fast once!

Governments create economic inefficiencies by prioritizing wealth distribution and central planning over personal freedoms. Without a profit motive, people's incentives for innovation and productivity gradually disappear. When you mess with incentives and the pricing mechanism of the free market, resources get misallocated, and shortages inevitably follow. Distorting market signals with interventionist policies deprives producers of their only tool for assessing what to produce and in what quantities — the price signal.

Moreover, the administration of an interventionist economy requires extensive bureaucracy. Expanding governmental control leads to inefficiencies and a cumbersome regulatory environment, stifling entrepreneurship. No one will attempt to jump if the bar is set too high. The bureaucracy eventually becomes so convoluted that it hinders the very objectives it was meant to achieve, such as improving welfare or streamlining distribution. As Oscar Wilde said: "The bureaucracy is expanding to meet the needs of the expanding bureaucracy."

If a politician's goal is equality, infringements on people's personal freedoms and individual rights are unavoidable. Efforts to enforce equality result in a lack of recognition for individual effort and achievement, demotivating individuals from striving for excellence and leading to a cultural atmosphere where mediocrity is encouraged. You cannot achieve equality without sacrificing quality.

All redistribution schemes are costly affairs. They do not fall to their marginal cost of production since governments compete in producing "bads" rather than goods. Worse, the process becomes more costly over time and is not easily reversed. If you punish excellence and encourage mediocrity, mediocrity is what you'll get.

Entrepreneurs with political connections are better positioned to influence policy-making processes, potentially leading to regulations that favor their business interests. Lobbyism is everywhere, and politicians are treated to "free" lunches, breakfasts, and dinners all the time. The politically connected entrepreneur can advocate for beneficial tax policies to shape industry standards that disadvantage new entrants or competitors lacking similar political ties. Lobbyism is a fancy way of saying corruption.

At the end of the day, politicians, lobbyists, and bureaucrats are merely human beings. When they lie, plot, and scheme, they do so because of their incentives. Unfortunately, this behavior catapults you to the top of the democracy ladder. It's not so much that absolute power corrupts absolutely; rather it attracts those already absolutely corrupted. Being sociopathic is advantageous.

Despite its inherent flaws, democracy is often called "the worst form of government except all the others that have been tried." This argument omits that democracies grow more and more totalitarian over time and aren't necessarily sustainable. Modern democracy itself is a relatively recent phenomenon, historically speaking, and most of us are probably too optimistic about its robustness over extended periods. But this is not a book about the pros and cons of democracy. It's a book about why things are the way they are and why increasing your freedom footprint makes the world a better place. We live in a world where most governments are growing, not shrinking. In such a world, pleasing bureaucrats becomes increasingly profitable, while providing as much value as possible to your fellow man becomes increasingly futile. This is Clown World™.

At the time of writing, Clown World is still in full swing and shows few signs of slowing down. Claudine Gay has recently stepped down from her position as president of Harvard University after being accused of plagiarism over fifty times. Still, the public debate is not about how this could happen in one of the world's most renowned universities but rather about whether letting her go was racist or not. A new law compels all federally regulated employers in Canada to stock "free" feminine hygiene products in all restrooms, including men's rooms. A new Star Wars movie is in the works at Disney, directed by a Pakistani feminist lady with virtually no previous directing experience, and the live-action remake of Snow White (played by a not-so-snow-white actress) came very close to having no dwarves in it whatsoever. On top of this, some transsexual men splashed onto "Women of the Year" lists in several fashion magazines last year. All in the name of diversity, equity, and inclusion. As I pen these words, my politically correct word processor suggests I use another word than "transsexual" because some people may find that particular word offensive. At the same time, there's a war in Ukraine and another in the Gaza Strip, and the official inflation number for several Western countries is in the double digits. How did it come to this?

Why on Earth are people still getting upset over people's genders and skin color shortly after almost all Western governments forced us to inject a poorly tested experimental drug into our arms, made our kids wear masks in school, and let big multinational conglomerates violently grab monopoly positions in their respective industries by forcing every mom-and-pop store to close and run out of business?

Of course, there's an answer to all of this, which is more straightforward than you might think. When the money stops working, everything becomes political and a farce. The urge for a free lunch got us here, and we're about to be forced to pay the damn bill anyway, with interest.

Bitcoin offers a solution to all of it. When you have non-confiscatable money that anyone can teleport anywhere on the planet at a tiny cost, you can bypass most, if not all, of Clown World. A business no longer has to be a bureaucratic entity; it can simply be a chat group. Bitcoin doesn't, and more importantly, cannot care about borders and regulations as long as you don't convert it back into fiat.

Bitcoin is still in its infancy, and most bitcoiners and Bitcoin businesses are still forced to convert back to fiat now and then. We live in a transitory phase, and things such as Bitcoin ATMs will look as ridiculous as phone booths in the not-too-distant future. But it's not only the ATMs that will fall into obsolescence. Everything in the Jurassic fiat currency world is on the brink of extinction. Are you a dinosaur or a human being?

Slay Your Heroes

Imagine a world where honesty and integrity reign supreme — a world of true individual sovereignty. Does this sound like a utopian fantasy? This parallel reality is already unfolding for those who have embraced the Bitcoin revolution.

Spend time in the Bitcoin community, and you'll glimpse this better future — an environment where people carry themselves with palpable confidence, freed from the shackles of endless financial stress and status anxiety. The superficial need to posture and conform melts away when you understand that Bitcoin provides you with a secure, self-sovereign monetary future.

This is the transcendent promise of Bitcoin — not just a novel currency but a complete paradigm shift that upends society's coercive institutions and returns power to the individual. Emancipation reverberates outward from those who have transcended fiat's distortions and awakened to this new economic renaissance. When people know enough about Bitcoin to have stopped worrying about their financial future, they usually care less about how others perceive their words and actions and more about honesty and integrity. Of course, this is only true for actual bitcoiners and not those who haven't yet accepted this new reality — those still in it for the fiat gains.

The first decade of Bitcoin's existence was an era of separating the wheat from the chaff — figuring out who had integrity and who didn't. The buzzword salad of the "wider crypto industry" wasn't particularly beneficial to anyone. Nothing burgers almost always come with a free side dish of word salad. More than a decade post-inception, some of the words in these charlatans' outdated narratives still linger but now act as an instant red flag. As we move deeper into hyperbitcoinization, it becomes increasingly easy to detect lies. Nowadays, only if you have been living under a rock for the last ten years would you fall for snake-oil salesman jargon like "crypto," "blockchain technology," "Web3," or "Decentralized Identity."

If you've attended Bitcoin events over the last ten years, you know how depressingly large the proportion of scammers can be when the topic is money itself. Some conferences, attended by people looking for a quick buck, have been fertile ground for swindlers and buzzword-mongers. However, as the so-called industry evolves, the number of dishonest people at Bitcoin events diminishes. A signal is emerging from the noise. Nowadays, Bitcoin-only events are more common and attract more ethically aligned people. But there are other trends, too.

The first generation of bitcoiners were the cypherpunks. They were defiant, intelligent, and, more often than not, quite disagreeable freedom-loving shadowy super-coders dreaming of ways to rebel against everything. The Silicon Valley move-fast-and-break-things types came next. With them came the "alt-coins," which allegedly could do everything from executing legal contracts to tracking banana shipments. As Bitcoin has grown more mature and mainstream, the bad seeds have mostly been weeded out, but the cypherpunk ideals that launched the movement are fading. Some would even claim that the community is not as intelligent as it used to be.

We live in a time when social media algorithms largely determine who gets attention. If you want others to hear your ideas, you must, at least partially, participate in these attention games. Even if being listened to isn't necessarily your goal, you still need *some* recognition to get the opportunity to connect with the right people. Being well-connected has always been valuable, but this has never been as obvious as in the internet age. Likes and reposts get you a long way, regardless of what career you're pursuing. People at Bitcoin events are somewhat resistant to these forces, but they are not immune.

We all play games to some extent. We use means, including our brains and other communicational organs, to reach our ends. The marginal utility of an additional powerful friend is always high. Conversely, the marginal utility of money derives from the additional consumption it finances. Therefore, the marginal utility of money diminishes at a slower pace than other goods. The same is true for human connections. Spending time making new friends is almost always worth the effort, especially if the friends we make are honest, pleasant to be around, and well-connected. Metcalfe's Law applies to nearly everything in human affairs — the value of a communications network is proportional to the square of its number of connected users.

So, what is honesty? We've all encountered the overly agreeable type who only wants to connect with you because there's something in it for them — people who default to agreeing for the sake of agreement — the fairweather friend. We've also encountered those who default to contrarianism and never agree to anything. So, who's more honest, and how would you know? Can people be manipulative without even knowing they are? How do you distinguish between diplomacy and ass-licking?

American poet and civil rights activist Maya Angelou once famously said, "When someone shows you who they are, believe them the first time." This advice is sound, regardless of whether we talk about good or bad actors (or Ms. Angelou herself for that matter). When people show you, through their actions, what they are willing to do for others or (perhaps more importantly) to others, you'd better pay attention. Sure, a blind hen can find a golden pebble, and people make mistakes, but hiding one's true character as the years pass is challenging. In line with the tit-for-tat strategy from game theory, giving people the benefit of the doubt, more often than not, is usually a good idea. Forgiveness and second chances are powerful. Third chances are not. As George W. Bush once famously declared, "Fool me once, shame on... shame on you. Fool me... you can't get fooled again."

Your time on this Earth is limited. To make the most of it, surround yourself with people who make you better. Curate your friends, and whenever you can, curate your coworkers, too. Some say you are the average of the five people you spend the most time with. Whoever those five happen to be will change over the years. At first, they're your parents and grandparents. Then they're your siblings and friends, and after you start a family, your spouse, kids, and coworkers play a more prominent role in your life. These changes are gradual and flow with the sands of time. Your personality is colored by your genetics, too, of course. For instance, your intelligence and temperament are relatively fixed traits you are born with and can't do much about. Focus on what you can, and shift your attention to those who share your values.

The Internet is the most fantastic computer game ever created. It has morphed the entire planet into a life-imitating-art-imitating-life sandbox-style role-playing game of epic proportions. Like in any regular RPG, players are born with predetermined physical and mental traits.

They acquire skills, unlock achievements, and level up their character as the game progresses. There's no specific goal to the game, but there are a bunch of new areas to unlock, side quests, and storylines to explore.

Viewing the world in this way might seem cynical, but gamifying life doesn't necessarily mean manipulating people. In a computer game, you can use cheat codes and beat the game way too fast, but there's little to no satisfaction in doing so — this is also true in life. Unethical actions invariably backfire, never giving the actor the satisfaction they envisioned. Contrary to what Hollywood might have told you, psychopaths aren't happy but rather in a state of perpetual emptiness. Happiness is a byproduct of being useful to others. So, from a philosophical viewpoint, cheating doesn't work. Still, knowing what the game is and how to achieve specific goals is, like all other knowledge, never a heavy burden.

So, who is the greatest player of the Internet RPG of all time? Who's the GOAT? Arguably, no one's done it better than Satoshi Nakamoto. This guy (yes, in all likelihood, Satoshi was a guy) pulled off a reverse Leroy Jenkins moment that will never be surpassed in terms of sheer epicness. He created the best form of money humanity has ever experienced and then performed the greatest act of economic self-sacrifice of all time. All within less than half a decade. On April 23, 2011, Satoshi said he had "moved on to other things" and that "[Bitcoin's] in good hands with Gavin and everyone." He disappeared entirely after this, except for a brief March 7, 2014 message: "I am not Dorian Nakamoto."

Almost everyone agrees that Bitcoin wouldn't be the same without Nakamoto's selfless exit. Achieving true decentralization in a computer network with economic incentives is exceptionally challenging. It wasn't until August 2017 that any form of objective evidence of Bitcoin's users being in charge of the project could be detected when they denied the proposed SegWit2x hard fork.

Contrary to how outside observers might have perceived it, the "Block Size Wars" of 2017 were ultimately about control. The narrative pushed by those who sought to gain control of the network was that increasing the block size limit to accommodate more transactions would reduce settlement delays and individual transaction fees. Advocates for larger blocks, including prominent Bitcoin businesses and mining companies like BitPay and Bitmain, argued that this was necessary to foster Bitcoin's use as a peer-to-peer electronic cash system for everyday transactions, ensuring Bitcoin's practical use on a larger scale. They left out of the argument that increasing the block size limit would have set a precedent for doing so again, ultimately resulting in a timechain too large for regular people to download and maintain. Increasing the block size would have effectively sacrificed decentralization for scalability, as the cost of running a full node would grow too high for everyone except these large companies. In addition, it would have sent a signal to the market that the big players were in charge — not the users.

Fortunately, the big blockers lost the war, and a different solution — Segregated Witness (SegWit), which optimized the data structure of transactions without directly increasing the block size — was implemented instead. SegWit was a soft fork, meaning that nodes weren't forced to implement it, as they would have been in the case of the suggested block size increase. SegWit increased transaction capacity without altering the block size and facilitated second-layer solutions like the Lightning Network. Significantly, the inability to reach a consensus on increasing the block size directly resulted in the split of Bitcoin Cash from Bitcoin. Bitcoin Cash instantly increased its block size to 8 MB.

At the time of the split, one Bitcoin would buy you five Bitcoin Cash tokens, and many bitcoiners seized the opportunity to increase their stacks by selling the fake coins right away. In hindsight, this laughable attempt at replicating the discovery of resistance to replicability can be seen as a cross between a train wreck and a Christmas present to non-regarded people. The episode underscored Bitcoin's resilience and the importance of a conservative approach to protocol changes. Preserving a high degree of decentralization is paramount for Bitcoin’s security, which itself is upheld through community-driven consensus. Resistance to change is intertwined with Bitcoin's value proposition, and during the aftermath of the Block Size Wars, the market solidified its preference by adopting the fork that altered the protocol the least.

We don't know what Satoshi's stance in the Block Size Wars would have been, but we can guess. After all, he was the one who introduced the block-size limit in the first place. Regardless of whether he would have been for or against the SegWit2x proposal, his opinion would have inevitably influenced the views of others. Simply by weighing in, he would still have been in charge, and the network would have been under his control and, therefore, not decentralized. The emergence of decentralization is thus path-dependent. If you use a towel before you shower, you get a different result than if you use it after. Both Satoshi's disappearance and the outcome of the Block Size Wars were pivotal moments in Bitcoin's history. They are part of why the system works.

Self-proclaimed Bitcoin gurus come and go, and over the years, we've seen many let their egos get the better of them. If you look at the "cast" of a Bitcoin movie like *The Rise and Rise of Bitcoin* from 2014, you'll be amazed at how many of these early adopters have turned to the dark side. Some now run shitcoin casinos (otherwise known as "crypto exchanges"). Some have started shitcoin projects of their own, and some have just disappeared into obscurity after public embarrassment. Several have, of course, made massive amounts of money duping innocent people and selling fake bitcoins over the years. It's easy to see why so many have fallen for the temptation to exploit their influence. Caution: you can only sell your soul once — no refunds, no do-overs.

The first big wave of bitcoiners was mainly orange-pilled by one man: Andreas Antonopoulos. Because of Antonopoulos' excellent talks and appreciation from the community, bitcoiners shied away from challenging him when he published *Mastering Ethereum.* With a 70% pre-mine and an early roll-back of its supposedly immutable blockchain, Ethereum was an obvious scam from the get-go. Its relatively recent move to so-called "Proof-of-Stake" further cements its scammy nature. Still, the Ethereum foundation has been able to fool numerous "investors" over the years through buzzword-salad jargon, vaporware, and books like Antonopoulos' *Mastering Ethereum.* The decision to write a technical book about how to "use Ethereum" was, in hindsight, an obvious oopsie. Yet, no one dared to question anything Antonopoulos did for quite some time. Eventually though, all questionable moves get called out, and Mr. Antonopolous was not immune to the fierce criticisms of the cyber hornet swarm. Integrity is paramount to longevity in the Bitcoin space.

One iconic early adopter that no one dares to question is Satoshi Nakamoto himself. And for good reason! If anyone deserves idol status, it's Satoshi — the embodiment of selfless sacrifice. Right? Many, if not most, bitcoiners think so. Some even view Satoshi and the birth of Bitcoin as the second coming of Mr. Jesus Josephson! It's a convincing narrative that widens the gap between Bitcoin and shitcoins even further, helping people understand the crucial differences better. Right? *Right?!?*

While it is certainly possible (and even probable) that Satoshi sacrificed himself for the greater good of humanity, this assumption is far from unproblematic. Only Satoshi himself knows why Satoshi did the things he did. He most certainly believed that his actions would remove some felt uneasiness, but we have no idea what that felt uneasiness was. Moreover, we have no way of knowing if his disappearance was intentional. For all we know, he might have drowned, been run over by a combine harvester, or had a fatal run-in with Garth Brooks. He might also have realized that disappearing was necessary for Bitcoin to catch on but then continued to mine or stack anonymously for years. We simply do not know.

Personality cults are dangerous, and the Cult of Satoshi is no exception. When Craig "Faketoshi" Wright claimed to be Satoshi in 2016, many believed him. If you are Satoshi, proving you have access to Satoshi's private keys is trivial since all you have to do is sign a message. Despite refusing to verify his proclaimed identity, Wright managed to acquire a substantial following. He called his shitcoin "BSV - Bitcoin Satoshi's Vision" and likely made a ton of money scamming people with it. BSV was a train wreck on top of a train wreck, as it was a fork of "Bitcoin Cash," the original piece of cryptographic fecal matter residue from the Block Size Wars in 2017. Wright even sued a handful of prominent voices in the space, and only recently did he decide to drop charges in the face of overwhelming evidence and admonishment by a court that he had been faking it all along.

The danger in worshipping Satoshi as some kind of superhuman martyr lies not only in the risk of him being able to influence the network too much in case of his return but also in the danger of placing too much weight on the words he wrote while still active. Polymath or not, he was almost certainly a human being (or a few of them), and human beings are flawed creatures who sometimes make mistakes. If we take Satoshi's words too literally, we might deprive ourselves of the ability to fix critical issues with Bitcoin. Immutability is crucial to Bitcoin's survival, and any narrative threatening its decentralization is inherently dangerous.

Any portrayal of Bitcoin as something other than damn near perfect money risks sacrificing the golden goose for a Kinder Egg. If you are lured by thoughts of yield, rare sats, smart contracts, or "alternative use cases" for the blockchain, see it as a test of your resolve. Bold curiosity and critical thinking are the powerful mental tools that brought you here. Remember them, and remember that you cannot replace them with fairy tales, blind conviction, or appeals to authority. An open mind is only useful if it's intellectually honest. People will inevitably come along and try to put stuff in it, so make sure you fix your filters if you need to.

How you respond to Bitcoin's calling is entirely up to you. Various gurus, mentors, and semi-professional think-bois may be able to point you in the right direction, but in the end, you are the only one who can heed the call. This particular quest is yours and yours alone. It will, however, require you to de-program yourself and re-evaluate many, if not most, things you used to take for granted.

Do not trade Bitcoin for fiat gains! Thousands of YouTubers and other influencers will try to "teach" you how to interpret market movements, read graphs, and decipher what miscellaneous tea leaves are trying to tell you. It's all a trap. You don't need to learn how to trade Bitcoin. You need to learn how to *not* trade Bitcoin. Bitcoin only needs to keep working for "financial advisory" to become the most redundant profession in the universe during the coming century. Get your hands on as many sats as possible, and don't sell them. It's that simple. It's all the advice you will ever need. You're an absolute winner if you have one more Satoshi this year than last. Zoom out and be patient. Sell your chairs, slay your heroes, and take responsibility for your actions. In other words — stay humble and stack sats.

Hill-To-Die-On Picking

Welcome to the circus of mass delusion, where the ringmasters of fiat finance have us feverishly juggling manufactured crises and false partisan feuds. In Clown World, we're kept frantically pivoting between conveniently bifurcated "societal problems" that, in reality, are nothing but disagreements over the slices of an imaginarily limited economic pie. The great sleight-of-hand distracts us from the reality that true wealth is not a zero-sum game with winners and losers. We're trapped in a perpetual cycle of scarcity paranoia, and turmoil by design to prevent us from realizing our true potential. Yet nothing concocted in this deranged sideshow is worth sacrificing our grip on the truth.

Clown World is a direct result of the politicized fiat economy, which makes people focus on totally arbitrary issues. More frequently than not, the perceived "societal problems" in Clown World aren't even problems at all—unless you believe the economy is a zero-sum game, which it isn't. A fundamental mistake in economics is assuming that one person's success necessarily comes at the expense of another.

Take the perceived wage gap between the sexes, for instance. Why would this be a problem for anyone? What real-world suffering would such a statistical discrepancy cause?

All wages, hence all wage gaps, result from several lifetimes' worth of decisions by an aggregate of individual actors, making any comparisons of individual salaries futile. Even if two people hold the same position at the same company, it's entirely possible that they would have different salaries, and it's impossible to tell whether their wage gap is justified. Who has the authority to dictate how much compensation someone deserves based solely on what others happen to earn?

The debate about the wage gap between men and women is a fascinating example of arbitrary outrage because there are so many rampant misconceptions about the topic. First, humans are not very good at understanding exponentials. If a person works in a field and does a specific job over long periods, the increase in the value output from performing the tasks the job entails isn't necessarily linear. More likely, the impact is exponential. If an entrepreneur makes 100% profit per annum, he could double the size of the business every year, making the company's growth curve exponential. A similar logic applies to many other jobs. But, if a person's career is interrupted by a long break, such as injury, illness, or maternity, the compounding process is halted, giving a massive advantage to those who continue to work uninterrupted.

Further, women are generally more agreeable than men, affecting salary negotiation outcomes. From an evolutionary perspective, there's nothing strange about this agreeability difference. Female mammals have mammary glands, which makes them the primary baby feeders. Baby feeding reduces mobility, forcing females to "stay at home" more, regardless of which mammal we're discussing (except for maybe hyenas). By contrast, male primates generally are more mobile and have more muscle mass, and human males even require less sleep, making them more suitable for tasks like spearing down a mammoth and bringing it home in time for Mother's Day.

The Industrial Revolution opened up new career paths for women beyond traditionally feminine roles as more professions emerged that did not require physical labor. But should as many women as possible pursue engineering careers just because they can? That decision should, of course, be up to the individual woman. Yet, in circumstances where women have a choice, data indicates most women opt against pursuing engineering careers. In more developed regions (like Scandinavia, for example), where women can more freely choose what kind of life they want to live, they are more likely to choose more classically female professions such as nursing, teaching, or child care. In less developed countries (like India or China), the opposite is true. Women in these regions generally take on male roles because of necessity, not choice. In China, the self-inflicted demographic issues stemming from the one-child policy have created a scenario where there are fewer women than men, leading to the only-child women surviving the government mandates having to carry the entire burden of supporting the family. These women "choose" more male-oriented jobs, too. If there are no men around to hunt the mammoth, the women will have to. If they don't, the flock dies.

Nursing, teaching, and child care are all honorable jobs that need to be carried out by someone in the flock. But none brings home the metaphorical mammoth, without which the flock will perish! The ones who *do* bring home the mammoth are typically happy to share it, but suggesting that jobs that do not put mammoth burgers on the table are somehow as essential for survival as those that do is preposterous.

Comfortable outsourcing protection, women tend to vote more to the left than men. Seduced by the state's promise of a free mammoth salad for lunch, these women forget that freshly caught, neatly butchered, and perfectly cooked mammoths don't just appear out of thin air. In doing so, they replace the alleged abusive patriarch of the husband with the actual abusive patriarch of the state by voting for more "equality," which always equates to more taxes and more market interventions.

Politicians, especially those of the left-wing variety, often manage to make people think that equality of outcome between the sexes should be the norm. There's nothing natural about equality, though. Forcing people to pursue careers they aren't naturally drawn to or distorting the natural compensation discrepancy between mammoth hunting and elder care can only lead to a lower net outcome for everyone involved. Clown World begins with interventionism.

Of course, politicians love having women in the workforce because this means more taxes for them. This is also why politicians love "equality" in general. The only way for a third party to make anything more "equal" in society is to reduce everyone to the level of the lowest common denominator. A person who spends whatever they can get their hands on as fast as possible will never achieve anything, and you cannot make others more "equal" to this person by any other means than reducing everyone else to the same level. You can't fight poverty by fighting prosperity. Equality, regardless of whether it's equality of outcome or equality of opportunity, is not only impossible to achieve but highly immoral to even strive for. Equality before the law is thus the only ethical form of equality.

Even if something appears free, there is always a cost somewhere, whether hidden or overt. Politicians promote "free" healthcare, education, or other services to gain favor with voters, but these policies involve fiscal trade-offs and economic consequences that someone must pay for. Every decision has an opportunity cost — choosing one thing inevitably means giving up another. From "gender equality" to "free health care" to "carbon neutrality," someone will have to foot the bill at some point. That someone is you, the taxpayer.

The notion that group identity or group belonging bestows entitlements is complete Clown World nonsense. Consider the claim that a particular group is under or overrepresented in a specific field. The person declaring one group "victims" without any actual crime (not even a victimless one) having been committed is fueled by the desire for there to be a free lunch. At its core, the allure of the free lunch stems from a delusional sense of entitlement to others' resources.

The perceived problems stemming from different outcomes arising from different life choices and circumstances are everywhere, and the political measures proposed to "correct" these "issues" are increasingly preposterous. From a first principles perspective, there is only one human right, and that's the right to be left alone. It's the only right that can always be true for every person, regardless of where or when they are born. Every other so-called right necessarily violates this most basic right for someone else. If housing is a human right, this has to apply to people who can't afford a house. In turn, someone else's right to be left alone must be violated because someone has to pay for the damn thing.

Here, it's crucial to distinguish between the terms "lawful" and "legal." This distinction is vital in the context of legal philosophy and the understanding of the law's role and legitimacy in society. Let's explore!

A "lawful" act refers to an action or conduct following natural law or the first principles of justice and morality. It implies a universal standard of behavior that respects the rights and dignity of all individuals. In contrast, the term "legal" pertains to actions or conduct that comply with laws made by a legislative body or government. These are "positive" laws, meaning they are formally enacted and codified by authorities. The notion of "legal" implies something adheres to the rules set forth by a particular legal system at a specific time and place — nothing more, nothing less. Legal standards can change as governing bodies make, amend, or repeal laws. In other words, something legal is not necessarily lawful.

Circumstances where an act is legal but not lawful are everywhere. The very notions of taxation and inflation are legal but not lawful since they violate man's inherent right to be left alone. Conversely, actions that might be considered lawful (just and moral) but not legal (prohibited by statutory law) are even more abundant in Clown World.

Victimless crimes are punished every day in the Western world. In 2022, 400 people in Russia were arrested for things they said on social media. In the UK, the equivalent number was around 3300. The further away a society's legal system strays from fundamental property rights, the less lawful it becomes.

Frank Van Dun, a Belgian philosopher and classical liberal natural law theorist, examined the distinction between lawful and legal in his 1983 writing, *Het Fundamenteel Rechtsbeginsel* (*The Fundamental Principle of Law*). Van Dun argued that a rationally convincing answer to "What is law?" can only be found by respecting dialogue and argumentation. Thus, he is an adherent of argumentation ethics, further explored in the works of Hans-Herman Hoppe. Argumentation ethics establishes the consensualist ethic of non-aggression (the principle that aggression against the person or property of others is always unjust) as a presupposition of argumentation itself and, therefore, as a norm that anyone engaging in discourse must accept.

Imagine you're in a classroom where everyone tries to decide what game to play during break time. The students begin to suggest games, pointing out which would be the most fun. By talking and listening to each other, the students have all agreed to a few crucial rules without even uttering them.

Together, they are using words to figure things out, not pushing or hitting each other to get their way. It is as if there's an invisible rule that says, "We solve things by talking, not fighting." Simply put, they all agree to the non-aggression principle.

By discussing, they also agree that everyone should be able to speak up and have their ideas heard. It's like saying, "Everyone here is important, and everyone's ideas matter."

Imagine someone in the middle of this discussion saying, "Actually, I think it's okay to take what I want from others, even if it means hurting them." By joining in the talk, they have already demonstrated that they believe talking is the right way to solve problems.

A statement like "I'll just take what I want" can never really be an argument. Arguing against the act of argumentation is, by definition, irrational. In simple terms, argumentation ethics tell us that by solving disagreements verbally, we all agree that being peaceful and letting everyone have their say is the best way to go. Anyone engaging in argumentation and not respecting the outcome of the discussion is effectively just a bully mocking his next victim.

Modern societies have strayed far from rigid consensualist ethics. Any freedom-loving person who wants to exercise their birthright to be left alone has little choice but to take matters into their own hands. The long and winding road to freedom never leads through the dense forest of obedience. Getting into trouble with the law can be unwise as this can severely affect your future freedoms. So, how can one find a way of life that is ethical rather than criminal while simultaneously avoiding falling victim to stupid victimless crime laws? The first skill needed is how to choose your battles wisely. You have to figure out which hills that are worth dying on.

Many battles, verbal and physical, are fought over fruitless causes. Make sure the hill you're prepared to die on has a valley worth living in beneath it. Finding something worth fighting for is what makes living worth dying for. So, how can you find your hill to stand your ground on? Most people never figure out the answer to this question.

The task at hand is nothing less than finding the meaning of life. The meaning of *your* life, to be more precise. Moreover, there are no objective ways of knowing who succeeds at this fundamental task. One thing is for sure, though — noise blurs your signal. Advertisers, politicians, journalists, teachers — most of these people distract you from finding your path. "Aging is an extraordinary process whereby you become the person you always should have been," David Bowie once said. But this is only valid for people who are true to themselves.

Being true to oneself seems straightforward enough, but the process can be made easier and quicker, given the right tools. All tools have the same underlying purpose — to save time. You will need a remarkably efficient noise-removal tool to even have a shot at finding the meaning of your life and becoming the person you were always meant to be. That tool is Bitcoin.

Bitcoin is the most incredible noise remover ever discovered. Why? Because Bitcoin is entirely truthful. The reason for this is simple yet elegant. In Bitcoin, the map defines the territory — not vice versa. Whatever happened in the timechain is unequivocally true from the perspective of the network. Once a valid block is found, it is there forever, and everything in that block is, by definition, truthful.

Finding your passion, your hill to die on, is one of the most rewarding things you can do with your life. Now, can monetary riches be your passion? Is becoming rich a fulfilling goal to strive for? Philosophers have debated this point for ages. The thing is, no one wants money for the sake of the money itself. We want what we think that money will buy us. Whether that something is material goods, fame, fancy friends, political influence, or a supermodel wife, money is never the end goal. It is merely a means to whatever that goal may be. If you honestly examine your soul's deepest desires, you most likely crave love, belonging, security, and little else.

Rather than bringing you closer to your soul's deepest desires, some possessions hinder you from reaching them. They end up owning you, not the other way around. The notion that your possessions end up owning you has a flipside — if you can rid yourself of the urge to own something, you own that urge. Ridding yourself of as many material cravings as possible is the best freedom-increasing life hack ever. The power of becoming a stoic minimalist who no longer cares about stuff is perpetually underrated.

Of course, people around you, like your family and friends, may not have come as far in their philosophical journeys as you have. In all likelihood, they're just as materialistic as the next guy. When you have a family to provide for and an employer to please, the game of materialism forces itself into your life to a certain extent. However, ridding yourself of material cravings is still beneficial because it gives you "truth goggles" through which you can view the world. You'll more clearly see how much everyone around you is a salesman.

Bitcoin is an excellent noise-remover in this sense because of its non-inflationary nature. When you know that the purchasing power of your money is likely to increase over time, you are less likely to spend it on frivolous things. As Tyler Durden explains in Fight Club:

> Advertising has us chasing cars and clothes, working jobs we hate so we can buy shit we don't need. We're the middle children of history, man. No purpose or place. We have no Great War. No Great Depression. Our Great War's a spiritual war... our Great Depression is our lives. We've all been raised on television to believe that one day, we'd all be millionaires, movie gods, and rock stars. But we won't. And we're slowly learning that fact. And we're very, very pissed off.

When practically everyone on Earth uses a monetary system based on a deceitful lie, everything else becomes a lie, too. Inflation is theft disguised as altruism, and it distorts all price signals, making all of us "work jobs we hate so we can buy shit we don't need." Inflation is the great tragedy of our generation and has been the tragedy of many other civilizations, too.

In the Roman Empire, a small silver coin, the Denarius, once held immense power. First minted around 211 BC, the purity and consistent value of the Denarius fueled Rome's economic engine for centuries. As time passed, the pressures of prolonged military campaigns and political instability began to drain Rome's treasury. Several Roman emperors debased the currency to fund their ambitious infrastructure projects and their wars. They gradually reduced the silver content of the Denarius, supplementing it with cheaper metals like bronze or copper. Strategic debasement initially remedied

Rome's financial shortcomings but ultimately brought the mighty empire to its knees.

As the silver content dwindled, so did the coin's value. Hyperinflation eventually ensued, severely destabilizing the Roman economy. The diminished value of the Denarius affected the morale and loyalty of the Roman legions. Their wages, paid in the weakened Denarius, could no longer buy what they once did. The decline was not limited to the military. Public trust in the Roman economy eroded alongside the Denarius' value, contributing to economic disparity. The wealthy invested in land and other assets, but ordinary citizens saw their savings diminish faster and faster over time. Sounds familiar, doesn't it?

Today, much of the economic hardship and erosion of purchasing power from inflation is exported from Western nations to developing countries with weaker currencies. As their currencies continuously devalue against stronger Western ones like the U.S. dollar, these countries are forced into a cycle of dependency, where they must import essential goods at ever-increasing costs while their exports remain undervalued and cheap on global markets.

Western monetary manipulation traps these nations in a never-ending story of curtailed growth and dependency on economically dominant countries. Slavery was never really abolished but morphed into the type of economic serfdom that developing nations are forced to endure today. Corrupt governments and vampiric International Monetary Fund (IMF) policies trap the people of the global South into working for minuscule wages as long as the dollar reigns supreme. Echoing historical colonialism, these policies often involve high-interest loans with strict austerity conditions, prioritizing debt repayment over other public spending.

Consequently, the global South effectively pays taxes to the US.

"Until the philosophy which holds one race superior and another inferior is finally and permanently discredited and abandoned, everywhere is war." Both Bob Marley and Sinead O'Connor have famously quoted Haile Selassie's immortal words in their music. Whether Haile, Bob, or Sinead truly understood why this is the case is questionable. The intricacies of banking cartels funding the military-industrial complex via fractional money lending practices and petro-dollar dominance leading to inflationary economic colonialism are not easy to understand (let alone say), which is part of why the scheme has worked for so long. Many feel something is off; few can identify and articulate what.

Essentially, the poorer you are, the more you pay. Think about that for a second. No one on Earth would ever vote for a policy that made the poor pay higher taxes than the rich. Still, this is the world we find ourselves in. Increased poverty is the inevitable outcome of democracy combined with central banking. People will vote for the politician who promises the most free lunches. Currency debasement creates the illusion of the free lunch, which it then adds to your tab via inflation's flipside — wage deflation.

Bitcoin fixes this — all of it. When no one can bake theft into the entire system via the money printer, the prices of all goods fall to their marginal costs of production. When they do, they more accurately reflect their true value. Therefore, bitcoiners are better equipped to understand the world than anyone else.

This truth-seeking apparatus incentivizes every Bitcoin holder to save rather than spend and to help bitcoiners and Bitcoin-oriented companies thrive. The implications are simply mind-blowing. If there ever was a hill worth dying on, this is it. Never before in human history has there existed anything remotely close to what Bitcoin promises. Fix the money, fix the world — it really is that simple.

Pendulum

T*he Pit and the Pendulum* is a short story by Edgar Allan Poe, first published in 1842. It is a harrowing tale of psychological horror and physical torture set during the Spanish Inquisition, told by an unnamed prisoner sentenced to a horrible death. The prisoner is bound to a wooden frame, with a massive, razor-sharp pendulum slowly descending from the ceiling. As the pendulum's sweep narrows, dread mounts - will the prisoner escape this diabolical execution, or will the blade inevitably find its mark? Poe's haunting narrative is a stark reminder that just as the pendulum's path oscillates between extremes, so too do human thoughts and societal movements careen wildly, propelling us toward potentially catastrophic consequences with every erratic pivot.

I once tacked Crispian Jago's "Venn Diagram of Irrational Nonsense" to a bulletin board in a meeting room of an old workplace of mine. The diagram is divided into four main categories: "Religion," "Quackery," "Pseudoscience," and "the Paranormal." Each category bubble contains subwords like *reincarnation*, *aromatherapy*, *chemtrails*, and *telepathy*. These main categories all overlap each other, but only one word sits in the middle, straddling all four types of nonsense — *Scientology*.

What I found amusing about my colleagues' reaction to the diagram was that every one of them pointed out at least one word that they believed didn't belong on the diagram. One person explained how astrology had predicted last week's events with at least 95% accuracy, and another claimed acupuncture had cured their skin rash. Not one of my co-workers agreed with the contents of the entire diagram.

Looking at the same diagram today, I realize that even I have some objections to it. First, I notice how *Bigfoot* and *moon landing denial* are both categorized under "Pseudoscience." The diagram has a burden-of-proof problem. The burden of proof of Bigfoot's existence lies with whoever claims that Bigfoot exists. Similarly, the burden of proof of moon landings befalls the institution that claims they happened — the National American Space Agency, NASA. If someone fails to find the evidence presented unsatisfactory, this does not necessarily make them believers in pseudoscience. Still, the "denial" angle ended up on the diagram.

Another word, located at the intersection between "Pseudoscience" and "Quackery," caught my attention — a word that has a different ring to it in light of recent events: *anti-vaccination*. Thrown around carelessly during the COVID-19 lockdowns, this word has lost its original meaning to a certain extent. People who think that every human should have the right to choose what substances they put in their bodies are now lumped together with people who believe vaccines cause autism and are a deliberate eugenics scheme orchestrated by the Illuminati. There is no nuance anymore.

Like many bitcoiners, questioning mainstream narratives lead me to adopt first-principles thinking and the Austrian method of deductive reasoning. But over the years, I've noticed how many bitcoiners throw the baby out with the bathwater and dismiss all empiricism as pseudoscientific.

This phenomenon is to be expected as humans tend to overcorrect for historical errors.

Clown World is all about overcorrection. "Anti-racism" is a prime example of humans admitting an ethical mistake and trying to correct it by running as far as possible in the opposite direction. Similarly, in the Bitcoin world, carnivory is on the rise as a correction to Klaus Schwab urging us all to "eat ze bugz." Doing the opposite of whatever the mainstream tells you to do is probably not the magic cure-all that will save humanity from itself. It's more akin to Poe's blade taking another swing. So, how can we navigate this new paradigm, and what's the correct approach to get us closer to the truth?

To further explore different methodological approaches to science (but mainly for a laugh), I once created a Venn diagram of my own with some help from my friend Giacomo Zucco. This diagram comprised three circles: deductive reasoning (first principles), "bro science," and systematic academic research. We labeled the intersection between deductive reasoning and academic research "game theory," the intersection between bro science and academic research "placebo medicine," and the intersection between deductive reasoning and bro science "politicians suck." Bitcoin ended up in the middle of the diagram.

Deductive reasoning, or first principles thinking, is a powerful method of problem-solving that involves breaking down complex problems into their most basic, foundational elements. The idea is to strip away the assumptions, conventions, and generalizations that often cloud our judgment and understanding. Instead of relying on existing solutions, analogies, or practices, you start with the first principles you know to be true — the underlying axioms. These facts are so fundamental they can't be deduced from anything else. You then construct your reasoning and solutions from the ground up, anchored in these base truths.

Anecdotal evidence, or "bro-science," refers to advice or information based on personal experiences, stories, or observations rather than scientific analysis. It is common in everyday conversations and can cover a wide range of topics, from health remedies and dietary tips to business strategies and life hacks. Anecdotal evidence is characterized by its subjective nature and personal context. It often reflects individual experiences, which can vary widely from person to person. One person's experiences do not necessarily extend to anyone else.

Systematic academic research (empiricism) is a methodical approach to investigating phenomena through observation, experimentation, and evidence-based analysis. It emphasizes collecting data through sensory experience and measurable evidence. Researchers formulate hypotheses based on existing theories, design experiments to test these hypotheses, and analyze the results. The key feature of the modern scientific method is the peer review process, where scientists anonymously examine each other's work, supposedly ensuring the quality of the research.

There's a big difference between "science" and "the science." Unfortunately, the latter currently dominates the media topography. Scientists act on incentives as much as everyone else, and the flow of money dictates what is to be researched and when. Several systemic issues plague modern academia and undermine its core mission of advancing knowledge. The relentless pressure to secure funding forces scientists to prioritize "grant-worthy" research over passion projects, leading to a proliferation of papers produced mainly to obtain grants.

Securing funding for research outside mainstream interests is exceedingly tricky. Grant reviewers favor projects that align with their established views or current popular trends, stifling innovation and hindering the exploration of unconventional ideas. University administrators control the distribution of funds and determine which policies are implemented. They usually focus on projects they believe will boost the university's rankings or attract external funding. Focusing on short-term goals and measurable results distracts from supporting more creative or unconventional research, mirroring the tendency for high time preference in Clown World.

Peer reviewers, who decide what gets published, also play a significant role in this gatekeeping process. They evaluate the quality and significance of research submissions but often favor established theories and methods over innovative ideas. Reviewers might also let personal biases influence their decisions. Everyone has an ego, including your university's critical race theory professor.

Moreover, the same "cancel culture" culture that has turned modern comedy into a non-offensive, humorless, politically correct word syrup increasingly stifles science, too. Mainstream media's tendency to parrot and amplify whatever those closest to the money printer say affects everything. The underlying forces stemming from everyone's incentive to get as close as possible to the currency spigot create an intricate maze of "hands that feed" that will inevitably punish any rebellious scientist trying to bite them. Properly incentivized, misaligned projects perpetuate and expand popular narratives.

The empiricist's general view is that the scientific method reigns supreme; thus, one can never establish the validity of any statement with absolute certainty. The map can never represent the territory to a full extent. They claim an absolute truth cannot exist. The best we can ever hope for is approximation (which is where the scientific method comes in to help us error-correct and comprehend the nature of things a little better.) However, as Hans-Herman Hoppe points out in *Economic Science and the Austrian Method*, this assertion is, *in itself*, self-contradictory. The statement "We can never know anything with 100% accuracy" can only be true if the statement itself is 100% accurate, which, in turn, would prove the statement wrong.

The three methodological approaches (deductive reasoning, bro-science, and systematic academic research) are more or less suitable for specific situations. Still, deductive reasoning is the only tool in the toolbox for understanding what is wrong with the other two. Let's explore totally non-controversial topic of climate science to illustrate this!

Since the 1950s, scientists have extracted and studied ice cores, primarily from Antarctica and Greenland. These cores, encapsulating ancient air bubbles, act as time capsules, allowing analysis of past atmospheric conditions and shifts in gas concentrations. Through this practice, scientists have reconstructed Earth's climate over the last million or so years, shedding light on the natural cycles between ice ages. They have detected an apparent spike in CO_2 levels since the Industrial Revolution, suggesting that humanity's use of fossil fuels is causing rising CO_2 levels. This analysis falls under the category of systematic academic research and is probably pretty accurate. There is little reason to believe that all climate scientists are inherently corrupt. The problems accompanying climate alarmism do not stem from the scientific study of how our planet works.

To clarify, the problem with climate research lies not in the research itself, but in the incentive structure following it. Most scientists agree that the data show an unnatural rise in global CO_2 levels over the past century. They also believe human activity to be the primary cause of this increase. Some scientists, but not all, think there is a strong connection between rising CO_2 levels and global average temperatures. Like anything involving the future, though, these are assumptions. The Earth is large, and the solar system is massive. There's a not-so-insignificant chance that these climate models are missing some unknown variables at play here. Still, for argument's sake, let's assume it's all true and that disaster looms around the corner because humanity consumes fossil fuels. Oughtn't our governments then decide that everyone on Earth should be forced to buy electric cars, use paper straws, and bring a cotton bag to the supermarket in the name of St. Greta the Unquestionable?

What can the different methodological approaches (deductive reasoning, bro-science, and systematic academic research) tell us about how to tackle the problem appropriately? Systematic academic research can help us identify a problem, but it cannot provide a clear path to solve it. There's no way to extract an ought from an is. Especially not if we're discussing a global problem whose solution requires everyone on Earth to change their behavior. Deductive reasoning can't tell us what to do either, but it can point out how most of the proposed political measures are counterproductive. Even basic bro-science can tell us that upset teenagers throwing paint at priceless paintings and irreplaceable historical monuments won't affect global temperatures very much at all, really.

The only way to discover fundamental, irrefutable truths that inform our opinions about a particular problem is deductive reasoning from a first principles approach. For instance, it can tell us why an increase of a nation's money supply will inevitably lead to more consumerism and resource misallocation. It can also tell us that politicians willing to do whatever it takes to stay in power are likelier to win elections. It is, therefore, in the politician's interest to implement short-term "climate cosmetics" policies that do more harm than good to the planet in the long run. If climate disaster looms, the last groups of people you would want in charge of tackling the issues at hand are politicians and bureaucrats.

First principles thinking is the most rigorous methodological approach to any subject because it strips away accumulated assumptions and addresses problems at their most fundamental level. By eschewing assumptions and approaching societal issues from their base elements, first principles thinking provides insights that address the core issues. Without first principles, it's virtually impossible to account for second-order effects. In short, this approach prevents you from trying to cure your cancer with a band-aid, which is what most "climate policies" do.

Bitcoin helps you remove the noise from your life but also lets you see how noisy everyone else's life is. When the money is broken, resource misallocation distorts every truth-seeking endeavor. Bitcoin helps you see why that is the case and how it happens. Still, there are plenty of mental traps for bitcoiners to fall into. Some traps are rooted in a misconception of what problem Bitcoin solves. Others lie in overemphasizing certain aspects of the protocol and thinking these can somehow solve personal issues, too. Take Proof-of-Work, for instance. Some bitcoiners' attitudes towards Proof-of-Work, in particular, are remarkably Marxist.

One could argue that Proof-of-Work should have been called Proof-of-Results all along. It's the results that matter, not the work. The amount of work carried out by Bitcoin miners (the repeated hashing of a candidate block while trying out different nonces) is suggested by the number of zeros at the beginning of the hash of each resulting valid block, but it is not *proven*. A miner might find a valid block on the first try (even though the odds of that are infinitesimally low) or mine forever and never be rewarded. The miners put in the work to find blocks and get paid in satoshis because they believe they will be able to make a profit by selling those satoshis later down the line — not the other way around. People don't buy Bitcoins because they appreciate the nation-sized power consumption of the network. They *do* buy Bitcoins because they're secure, censorship-resistant, teleportable, and finite. Proof-of-Work is costly, which is what secures the network. But it's not the costliness of producing blocks that makes the coins valuable; it's the security, the portability, and the finiteness of the coins.

Similarly, most of humanity's cultural accomplishments presumably required a massive amount of physical labor. The Colosseum of Rome, the Pyramids of Egypt, and the Great Wall of China took decades, if not centuries, to complete. But a lot of labor also went into burying the millions of landmines in Iraq, Cambodia, and Bosnia, but no one considers those wonders of the world. Karl Marx believed labor was inherently valuable and that man-hours were interchangeable. But one hour of vegan burger-flipping is not necessarily worth the same as one hour of rocket engineering. Similarly, some bitcoiners believe human progress is directly linked to how many kilowatt hours we consume, but in doing so, they confuse cause and effect. Mere work is not of any value; people find work valuable because of the results said work produces.

"Just work hard enough, and you will succeed in life!" This is the implied promise of Proof-of-Work (and The American Dream™). But working on things that nobody asks for is futile. Moreover, while hard work is a crucial element of any successful endeavor, it is not the only thing that matters and sometimes it isn't even the most important factor. Talent is something you're born with and is one of the most crucial elements of success in any field. The Beatles' entire career spanned a mere seven years, during which they released thirteen studio albums, broke several international album sales records, and changed the course of pop music forever. A combination of talent, luck, and hard work made this possible. But also long periods of relaxation and fun. If you watch Peter Jackson's excellent *Get Back* documentary series about how The Beatles made the *Let It Be* album, it is hard to miss that what they're doing in the studio doesn't look remotely like Proof-of-Work. It's more akin to Proof-of-Always-Goofing-Around. The importance of having fun and exploring unconventional ideas in any creative endeavor is undeniable, and The Fab Four knew this.

Results matter, and only you know how to achieve them. Some of the most impressive human achievements stem from creativity — not work. Creativity is a strange beast to tame, and everyone's version of it is different. The best creative work happens when the creator is in a "flow state," which no one can achieve while multitasking. Focus is critical, whether you're in a bluegrass band, drawing a comic book, or carving out a muppet version of Venus de Milo. Isolate yourself (or your creative group) in time and space as much as possible, and you'll have a chance to find something novel and beautiful. When you do, it will feel like you're not in charge but channeling something already in the room.

Benny Andersson of ABBA once described the creative process as sitting by the piano and waiting for the song to float by. Creativity is subconscious, so you cannot push yourself to be genuinely creative via a relentless work ethic. All you can do is try to relax and stay present in the moment. When the flow state finally arrives, enjoy every moment of it. Few things in life feel better than surrendering to an idea and pursuing it wherever it may lead.

One can only truly discover Bitcoin by understanding the problem it solves. When digging a little deeper into the issues of broken money, one starts to realize the jaw-dropping magnitude of the problem. This realization is where many bitcoiners succumb to the intellectual laziness of believing in whatever the most popular conspiracy theory is at the moment. But "doing your own research" isn't just randomly believing what some guy on the internet thinks. It means actually doing research. Be bold and use your brain, but don't overcomplicate or overcompensate as a substitute for true understanding. Doing so will only swing Poe's blade in the opposite direction. What you want the blade to do is stop swinging altogether so that it will fall flat on your belly and not cut you in half. Stay calm and focused. Wait and ask why. Don't feed any beast. As Terry Pratchett put it, "The trouble with having an open mind, of course, is that people will insist on coming along and trying to put things in it."

Bill Murray built an international acting career by not caring about others' opinions. He figured out that he performed best while calm, comfortable, and not overthinking things. Following your passion and gut instincts in a relaxed manner can not only be the key to a successful career but also to a fulfilling life. Realizing the value of staying grounded and being present can lead to remarkable things. Remember to enjoy the moment because it is the only thing there is. Master the pendulum. Life happens in the present, not in the past or future. Right now is all you have.

We Are All Satoshis

In an intricate dance of zeros and ones, our computers become windows (pun intended) to a world more easily grasped by human minds. Words, sounds, and graphics emerge as humanly accessible representations of the digital realm. Yet, beneath this facade, a stark truth prevails: our computers may identify as non-binary, but in reality, the zeros and ones are all there is.

Computers are nothing but fancy abacuses. They far surpass the human brain in the singular task of calculation, but that's all they do. Despite that, applied ultra-fast mathematics unlocks a universe of digital wonders — from music and movies to books and games. Computers herald an unprecedented age of extraordinary human experience. All the wonders of the Internet Era emerge from a simple series of on-and-off switches.

So, how does the Internet actually work? The Internet is a global network of interconnected computers that communicate with each other using standardized protocols. When you access a website, your computer sends a request through a series of routers and servers using the Transport Control Protocol (TCP), which directs the information to its destination using Internet Protocol (IP) addresses. This is called the TCP/IP protocol. The requested data, such as a webpage or video, is broken into small packets, sent over the network, and reassembled on your device. On top of TCP/IP operate several application layer protocols, such as HTTP for transferring webpages and SMTP for sending and receiving e-mails.

The problem with terms like "transferring," "sending," and "receiving" when talking about computers is that data never really moves. It is always copied from one device to another. The nature of communication (in general) is such that no entity can send a message without knowing it first — communication *is* replication. Everything is a copy of a copy of a copy. The fact that anyone can copy any data is what makes computing, in general, and the Internet, in particular, so powerful.

The missing piece of the internet puzzle — the one piece needed to make the transfer of human value expressions possible — is the existence of something that *cannot* be copied. That something is the satoshi. A satoshi is the only piece of data that cannot be replicated. Think about that for a while! Ordered correctly, the numbers "0" and "1" can represent all information that is and ever has been on all electronic devices that have ever existed, including all the data on the timechain. Still, satoshis cannot be copied.

So, how can something made up entirely of data (ones and zeroes) be uncopiable? It sounds impossible, and from most perspectives, it is. Every single part of what makes up the sum we call Bitcoin can be copied. The code running on every Bitcoin node, each block in the timechain, and every individual version of the mempool can be copied. Only the satoshi itself can not. The satoshis don't even "exist" individually. There are only unspent transaction outputs (UTXOs) — ledger entries representing how many satoshis a specific private key unlocks. A satoshi is more akin to a centimeter than a dollar since all it does is measure the size of individual UTXOs.

The groundbreaking discovery of Bitcoin shattered the presupposed boundaries of digital communication by introducing a revolutionary concept — a form of information with no physical mass akin to a unique, weightless, purely informational element without protons or neutrons — Element Zero.[1] In the Bitcoin universe, ownership is synonymous with knowledge; to possess a Bitcoin is to hold a secret. The private key is the ethereal gateway to that ownership, a secret that transcends the physical realm and resides solely in the human mind, ephemeral and intangible.

Here, it is crucial to differentiate between ownership and possession.

Ownership refers to the legal right to use, control, and dispose of property, often supported by law and documentation. It includes long-term rights like selling, leasing, or modifying the property. Ownership applies to tangible and intangible assets and remains valid even without physical contact with the property.

Possession, on the other hand, is characterized by having physical control or custody of an item, regardless of its legal ownership claim. Possession can occur legally without ownership, like in the case of rented goods, or illegally, like in the case of something stolen, where the thief possesses the item but does not own it. Possessors who are not also simultaneously owners have limited rights to use the property and are not authorized to sell it or make significant alterations

---

1. The concept of Element Zero is further explained in Knut's book *Bitcoin: Everything Divided by 21 Million.*

to it without the owner's consent. Ownership is a broad, legally recognized claim to a property, whereas possession is limited to the actual physical control of it.

In Bitcoin, this is tricky. You cannot truly own a Bitcoin since you cannot own information, which is all that Bitcoin is. You cannot possess a Bitcoin either because you can't physically possess information. Information is not tangible. In fact, the only thing that makes you value the private key to a Bitcoin address more than other information is knowing how impossible it would be for an attacker to guess it.

In essence, Bitcoin is validated through collective verification, a process enabled by each participant running the protocol's code. This act, usually termed "running a node," must be initiated by a human deliberately choosing to participate in the network. Therefore, the actual node is not the machine but the person — the keeper of secrets, the decision-maker. In this light, every individual in the Bitcoin network is a node, and the computers and applications involved are merely their calculation assistants.

Alongside vigilant noderunners, Bitcoin miners form another pillar undergirding the network's integrity. Bitcoin mining is often misconstrued as a process of solving complex math problems, when really it is essentially about guessing a number that satisfies a set of specific criteria. Even the specialized hardware unit used for mining, the Application Specific Integrated Circuit (ASIC), is a mere tool in this quest — a sophisticated abacus dedicated to repeatedly running a specific algorithm. Just as in the case of running a node, a real human being must deliberately decide to purchase the ASIC, plug it in, connect it to the network, start hashing, and eventually complain about the electricity bill. The real miner is the human behind the machine, choosing to engage in this digital lottery — not the ASIC.

The odds of a single mining machine finding a block are infinitesimally small, so miners usually connect to "mining pools" that harness the collective power of a whole bunch of individual miners' hardware to search for blocks together. Miners in a pool share their rewards based on the amount of work (hashing power) contributed. This collaboration allows for consistent earnings, as finding a new block and receiving the associated reward is ridiculously competitive and completely random. In this way, mining pools allow smaller miners (individuals) to participate in Bitcoin mining and receive regular payouts.

However, if a person decides to mine using a mining pool that isn't transparent and doesn't let the miner select their own block template, they're not really miners at all but merely hash power salesmen. In this case, the actual miner is the owner of the mining pool. More on this later. For now, let's turn back to the concept of ownership for a moment.

In Bitcoin, ownership is ultimately woven into human memory. If the seed phrase (or private key) of a Bitcoin wallet lives only in a person's mind, that individual becomes indistinguishable from the satoshis they own, which underscores a somewhat bizarre insight about Bitcoin's users: They are no longer mere humans but facets of the same, singular, interconnected entity. We are thus not "all Satoshi" (especially not you, Craig), but all of us (literally!) *are* our individual satoshis. So, in reality, Bitcoin is not really "backed by energy" but by human action and incentives.

The insight that we are all part of the same entity spawns a unique culture of cooperation and long-term thinking among bitcoiners. We are all incentivized to think long-term, save rather than spend, and help each other succeed.

Bitcoin, therefore, is more than a set of digital rules or a network of computers. It embodies a collective human agreement leading to a convergence of individual wills. It beacons peace in our complex world, illuminating a path toward cooperation and truth beyond the constraints of the fiat monetary paradigm.

The longer you've experienced Bitcoin and, by extension, other bitcoiners, the more pronounced this seemingly magical aspect of the network becomes. Considering our conclusion that we are all part of the same being, it all makes perfect sense. Something profoundly human is going on here. Bitcoin points out the obvious: We'll all be better off if we cooperate. This is what "removing the noise" is all about.

The actual decision-makers in Bitcoin are the noderunners. Those who run nodes. Most of them receive satoshis in exchange for goods, services, and sometimes, even dollars. Their primary concern is the immutability of transactions, ensuring that once they part with their product or service, the satoshis they receive remain in their wallet. Miners also play a pivotal role here by providing immutability as a service, embedding transactions into blocks in exchange for transaction fees. However, the system ensures that the receiver, the ultimate consumer of the immutability service (the noderunner) has the final say in validating Bitcoin transactions.

Contrary to some opinions, running a Bitcoin node does not directly contribute to network security. The number of nodes is, for the most part, irrelevant to those receiving Bitcoin. Likewise, hodlers (Bitcoin holders) have no real power in the protocol's power dynamics. You don't automatically get a say in Bitcoin's future merely because you sit on a large stack of sats.

At any time in general, and post-hyperbitcoinization in particular, the only way to derive value from your satoshis is to exchange them for goods and services. At the time of writing, MicroStrategy Inc. holds about one percent of the total supply of Bitcoin that will ever exist. The only way for the corporation to leverage this stack-size advantage over time is to spend them, spreading wealth across the network.

Bitcoin is unique in that the receiving party in a Bitcoin transaction decides what constitutes valid satoshis *to them*, akin to a retailer validating the authenticity of cash. This dynamic is evident in cases where variations such as the many forked versions of the Bitcoin code are involved. If a receiver doesn't recognize a transaction as valid, the transaction falls through.

Bitcoin operates as a market for immutable transactions. Its design inherently opposes state intervention, evident in its inability to be arbitrarily printed, its permissionless nature, and its resistance to centralized control. The state, including its banking system, aims to regulate monetary supply and maximize tax revenue. Bitcoin challenges the statist quo by providing a separate system where transactions can be anonymous and beyond state control. The separation of money and state is one of the core advantages of Bitcoin over traditional financial systems. In essence, Bitcoin wouldn't work if a lawmaker (or anyone else, for that matter) had the power to interfere with it.

As Bitcoin grows and threatens state objectives, governments may react by passing punitive laws and supporting regulatory attempts to control the protocol. This could lead to a bifurcation: a state-controlled 'safe' version of Bitcoin (essentially another form of fiat) and the original Bitcoin, which would operate underground. For this attack vector to be viable, state actors would have to collude and strategize effectively to bring down the protocol. Good luck with that!

Enter the CBDC. The abbreviation stands for Central Bank Digital Currency, a concept so blatantly Orwellian it hurts. In the wake of Bitcoin's success, the EU, among many other state actors, has begun positioning CBDCs as part of the brave new world. But a CBDC is not just another Bitcoin clone. It's a tool for governments to program and control their subjects.

In our current fiat system, you reveal sensitive information about your whereabouts and spending patterns whenever you swipe your debit card. A CBDC economy would introduce an extreme form of surveillance akin to a China-style social credit score system, with a level of scrutiny that would remove your humanity and turn you into a mere pawn on someone else's chessboard, ready to be sacrificed at any moment. The concept of "programmable people" emerges, where everyone's financial behavior can be completely controlled and manipulated. Transactions could be approved or denied based on compliance with predefined criteria, effectively programming your actions and decisions, stripping away any remnants of personal autonomy. You would essentially become a tool for enforcing powerful external agendas.

With the advent of CBDCs looming, Bitcoin faces more and more restrictions, and even criminalization. Fortunately, Bitcoin is designed to become more decentralized over time. As it grows, its architecture spreads risk across a greater number of participants, leading to a resilient network that thrives despite government attacks. Still, it's essential that as many participants as possible do their homework and start acting in Bitcoin's best interest. If you're a merchant, run your own node. If you're a small miner, don't connect to a pool that isn't transparent about its policies.

The importance of individual responsibility in Bitcoin cannot be stressed enough, and this applies regardless of your tier of technical expertise. Tech-savvy or not, the choice is yours. No spoon-fed compliance here; only you can decide to bite the hand that faux-feeds you. Mark your territory and heed the Beastie Boys' battle cry: You've got to fight for your right to party.

The flip side of the freedom coin is always responsibility, which is why security and convenience are mutually exclusive. For Bitcoin safekeeping, this is absolutely true, technically speaking. You, the user, are fully responsible for ensuring that your satoshis are actually yours, that the hardware you buy and software you choose to run aren't corrupt, and that your computer isn't infected by viruses or malware. But the tradeoffs between security and convenience aren't exclusive to the digital realm — far from it.

One could even argue that the fiat monetary paradigm took hold because most people opted for convenience over security. Again, the urge for there to be a free lunch rears its ugly head as the root of all evil. Benjamin Franklin advised: "They who can give up essential liberty to obtain a little temporary safety deserve neither liberty nor safety." One of my favorite computer games, *Civilization IV*, paraphrased this mantra: "Any society that would give up a little liberty to gain a little security will deserve neither and lose both," which, for the modern reader, is an even better way of putting it. It is important to remember that nation-states are not the only ones forced to make these tradeoffs. Each individual faces the trade-offs between liberty and safety, too. The convenient illusion of security is the more common choice, of course. If it wasn't, there would be no nation-states. Once again, this is hill-to-die-on picking. Is the jurisdiction you happened to be born into lawful enough for you to make the conscious decision to obey its laws or is rebellion on the table? No one but you can make these choices. Are you a criminal? Are you standing up to the Nazis? Only you can know.

I have a late friend who used to work for the Swedish Economic Crime Authority. I once asked him what percentage of the Swedish population would be categorized as economic criminals if they got caught. I wondered because Swedish economic law is complicated, and I suspected many of my fellow Swedes were committing felonies they weren't even aware of. Swedes are obligated to report virtually everything they do with their money, and proving their innocence falls on them. In Sweden, you're not "innocent until proven guilty" but "guilty until able to convince a jury that you're not." My friend paused for a moment then answered, "Everyone." Every Swedish soul is guilty of at least some economic crime.

It's not like Sweden is a particularly extreme jurisdiction. In some US states, judges own prisons and are paid for each new inmate they incarcerate, giving them an incentive to condemn as many suspects as they can. As an example of how corrupt and complicated international law can be, I refer to my dear friend, Mr. Hodlonaut the Norwegian Space Cat, who had more than three years of his life stolen by a wealthy narcissistic fraudster. Mr. Cat had to fight a legal battle in which it was clearly evident, even before the trial, who the actual perpetrator was.

As we've already explored, "equality of outcome" is a fallacy and one of the worst hills to die on since it can only be achieved by wing-clipping and impoverishing everyone to the maximum extent possible. What is more challenging to see, even for people on the right side of any political aisle, is that "equality of opportunity" is an equally vile goal to strive for since equally abhorrent measures would have to be instituted to achieve it. For the mirage of "equality of opportunity" to materialize, a nightmarish vision must unfold

- every newborn would have to ripped from its mother's arms at birth by the state and condemned to poverty at birth. Huxley's *Brave New World* and Orwell's *1984* loom as chilling premonitions. In these two fiction-as-blueprint books of the modern left, and in their slightly less fictional but equally disturbing antecedent, Marx's *Communist Manifesto,* perverse equality reigns while the human spirit is subjugated to cruel oppressions. Reminder: the only equality that is universally fair is equality before the law.

Bitcoin is the most potent oppositional force to "equality-focused" Clown World policies. The oppressed no longer have to choose between voting with their feet and escaping or standing their ground and revolting. Freedom seekers everywhere now have a peaceful way to opt out by adopting an entirely voluntary system, the long-term implications of which cannot be overstated. We're living through the early stages of a seismic paradigm shift in human existence — we are becoming our money.

Mind Over Matter

The bitter Gothenburg chill cut through my jacket as I sprinted down the slushy sidewalk, heart pounding. My boots slopped onto the pavement in a desperate rhythm, but it was no use — the bus pulled away, that smug driver glancing back at me in the rearview with a maddening smile. Another day, another failure to catch my chariot to class on time.

One day, I decided to stop. I promised myself never to run to catch any type of public transport again, except maybe an airplane. Enough is enough! I already hated the stressful nature of living in a big city, navigating grey slush and slippery ice patches every day (except for maybe two afternoons in summer when the universities are closed anyway). My constant failure to make the bus on time added unnecessary stress to my already busy schedule. Once the decision was made, I noticed a strange phenomenon — I stopped being late. Running was no longer an option, so I instinctively left the apartment earlier. The stress simply went away. Everything changed once I realized I couldn't change the weather conditions, let alone the bus driver's smugness. The only thing I could change was my attitude. One simple boundary altered my entire reality.

The extent to which the mind creates reality, and the validity of the objective-subjective dichotomy in general, are fascinating philosophical puzzles that raise questions about the nature of reality and its relation to our perceptions of it.

A good starting point in this exploration is Simulation Theory. With rapid advancements in technology, especially in computer graphics and Midwit Obsolescence Technology (AI), it's conceivable that future simulations could be indistinguishable from what we call reality. In short, humans and their machines are improving their reality-mimicking capabilities at a mind-boggling pace. So, how do we know we're not already living in a simulation? Whenever you're forced to complete a captcha on a website, a similar philosophical dilemma arises — if you were a robot, how would you know?

The simulation concept extends to Bitcoin's operation within a presumably simulated environment. Since a computer couldn't ever "fake" Proof-of-Work, the simulation would have to do the work itself, raising some intriguing questions: Could Bitcoin's Proof-of-Work mechanism influence or even slow down the simulation? Would the "avatars" living in this simulation be able to detect this regression? Would they feel it?

Recent developments in neurotechnology have seen brain cells integrated into computers to enhance our processing capabilities, further blurring the boundary between the human brain and our computational tools. Both our brains and our computers run on energy and electrical impulses, but our perception of and interaction with the world differ. Could artificial systems ever gain a sense of consciousness or feeling, something inherently human and beyond the capabilities of current AI technology? We may never know. From a praxeological perspective, however, machine consciousness make little sense.

As Mises teaches us, removing a felt uneasiness is the goal of every conscious actor's deliberate action. The actor envisions a future state in which they've performed an action and decides whether to act if that future state is preferable to the current one. No machine existing today can ever choose actions in this way since they have no means of feeling uneasy. In its current state, AI is thus provably lacking agency or free will.

Now, do humans have free will? Can we even make conscious decisions? And if so, what effect does the decision-making process preceding the actual synapses firing off in the brain have on our choices?

From a neurological perspective, the conscious part of your brain isn't in the driver's seat. Consciousness comes with about a 300-millisecond lag. The decisions you think you made, your brain already made for you before it made you feel like you consciously made the decision. You are not in charge; your brain is. To further blow your mind — you can't even control what thoughts come into your mind, or when. Our ability to deliberately do stuff is significantly limited. It's even difficult to prove that human free will extends beyond choosing what thoughts to pay attention to - what to focus on. What's even more inherently misunderstood by our minds is to what extent this focusing of the mind actually changes reality, not only your perception of it.

The famous quantum-mechanical "double-slit experiment" illustrates how observation can affect outcomes, suggesting that our observation might literally shape reality. In its simplest form, the experiment involves a light source that emits a beam of light (photons), a screen with two parallel slits, and a photographic plate or a screen to observe the light pattern beyond the slits. When light is shone on a screen with just one slit open, it behaves as expected; a single bright band is observed on the detecting screen, which is what you would expect to see.

Things become interesting when both slits are open. Instead of seeing two bright bands corresponding to the two slits (as one might expect if light were purely particle-like), an interference pattern of several bands emerges. This pattern resembles what you would see with waves interfering with each other - where peaks of waves align, you see bright bands, and where a peak and a trough align, they cancel out, suggesting that light behaves like ripples in the ocean of the quantum realm after they pass the slits. Perhaps even more surprisingly, even when electrons are fired one at a time, they still behave as if each electron goes through both slits simultaneously, like a wave interfering with itself. This result indicates that particles like electrons also exhibit wave-like properties.

The most bewildering aspect of the double-slit experiment arises when measuring devices are placed at the slits to observe which slit a particle goes through. When such measurements are made, the interference pattern disappears, and particles like they're particles again, producing two bands on the screen corresponding to the two slits. This suggests that observation or measurement "collapses" the wave-like behavior into a particle-like behavior. Perception literally interferes with reality.

So, if the photons and electrons around us change when we observe them, what about the electrons in our brains? Do our brains and consciousnesses choose which parts of reality to perceive and interact with, given that our brains are made up of these particles? Are we actively creating our experienced reality, and (if so) to what extent?

Consciousness is one of the great mysteries of nature — no one knows why it's there or where it came from. Since the days of Descartes, all we've been able to prove about consciousness is his a-priori conclusion: "I think, therefore I am." We subjectively experience whatever our senses feed us. A dog has a different experience of reality than a human, but each human most likely also experiences reality differently from every other human. The color orange looks different to each and every one of us. Probably. If this is the case, the so-called "Fermi Paradox" may have a new solution.

A concept in astrophysics and cosmology, the Fermi Paradox highlights the puzzling disconnect between the high probability of the existence of technologically advanced extraterrestrial life and the lack of evidence for such civilizations. The paradox is named after physicist Enrico Fermi, who famously asked, "Where is everybody?" during a casual conversation in 1950. Fermi noted that given the vast number of stars in the Milky Way galaxy, many of which are similar to the Sun and likely to have Earth-like planets, it would be reasonable to expect a significant number of intelligent civilizations to exist. Furthermore, given that some stars are billions of years older than our solar system, some of these civilizations could be far more technologically advanced than ours and capable of interstellar travel or communication. Bewilderingly, there's absolute radio silence out there, which implies no such civilizations exist.

The solution to Fermi's paradox may be simpler than we think. If objective reality is where our subjective interpretations of reality collide, the vast distances between interstellar objects might make "syncing" our realities with the realities of various xenomorphs impossible. What's really curious about this theory is that we can explain it using an intriguing concept in Bitcoin — the Hash Horizon.

If the nature of the universe is as subjective as quantum mechanics suggests, the "map defining the territory" concept in Bitcoin may be more similar to the actual universe than we think. The average time between each block in the timechain is ten minutes, meaning that a node more than ten minutes away from another node could not reliably sync with the network since it would be one block behind almost all the time. The "Law of Hash Horizons" states that the farther miners are from the "center of hash," the less effective their mining efforts become. The "center of hash" is a point near the center of the Earth, slightly closer to the continent on which most of the mining power currently resides.

Communication between Earth and Mars will require a sophisticated, laser-powered telecommunications network. Assuming our current understanding of physics remains the limiting factor, the signals sent will still take an average of 12.72 minutes due to Mars' distance from Earth's "center of hash." Martians will undoubtedly be able to use Bitcoin, especially via second-layer technologies like the Lightning Network, but they will face transaction verification delays due to their distance from Earth, creating unique security challenges.

Keeping your Bitcoin node synced with the majority of the network from Mars would be impossible for most of the Martian year. When your Martian node is busy validating transactions in block X, Earthling miners are already mining on block X+1 or even X+2. Mining Bitcoin on Mars will also be impractical for the same reason. The communication delays will prevent Martian miners from staying synchronized with the timechain, resulting in fewer successfully mined blocks. In all likelihood, Earth will forever dominate the Bitcoin mining industry, even as humanity expands into the solar system and beyond.

Launching another coin altogether would obviously be futile since whoever started the project would have insider information about Bitcoin. Absolute mathematical scarcity achieved by consensus in a sufficiently decentralized distributed network was a discovery rather than an invention. A network of participants aware of this discovery cannot achieve it again since the very thing discovered was resistance to replicability itself. Any duplicate, including Marscoin, would inevitably be doomed to evolve into yet another worthless shitcoin.

Here's the mind-dynamite part: What if the intersubjective nature of consciousness works similarly? If our minds define the territory by drawing the map of reality together, akin to how the Bitcoin network participants create their own territory by designing the timechain together, does this mean that consciousness has a hash horizon, too? If this is the case, the solution to the Fermi Paradox is simple — other life forms are too far away for us to sync reality with them. Our reality would fundamentally differ from theirs, as their minds would create other intersubjective realities within their hash horizons. Reality-syncing would only be possible within a particular area of spacetime.

Speaking of spacetime, let's think about our spatial and temporal dimensions from a more strict physics perspective. According to Einstein's theory of relativity, spacetime is a dynamic fabric around us that can be warped and curved by mass and energy. This curvature alters the paths objects take through space and time, which we perceive as the force of gravity. When a massive object, like a planet, a star, or a black hole, is present, that object distorts space and time around it. Other objects move along the curves of this distortion, which explains why planets orbit stars and why light bends around massive objects.

From a photon's perspective, time stands still because it travels at the speed of light. As an object approaches the speed of light, time dilation becomes extreme. For a photon moving at light speed, time dilation is infinite, meaning that time does not pass at all from the photon's point of view. Consequently, the photon experiences no passage of time between its emission and absorption, making its journey instantaneous in its own frame of reference.

Typically, we perceive time as a linear progression akin to a sequence of images, where each frame captures the universe at a distinct moment. This succession of moments feels intuitive, with the past fading and the future yet to unfold. The word "timeline" is an appropriate descriptor for this idea. A timeline is an arrow with the future toward the direction of the tip, a point representing the present in the middle of the arrow, and the past on the opposite side. However, this linear perspective is upended when considering the concept of a four-dimensional block universe. Let's explore.

The theory of relativity disrupts the traditional separation of time and space, merging them into a single 4D continuum known as spacetime. Movement through space is intrinsically tied to movement through time, leading to the realization that 'now' is relative. Moving at different velocities, observers will slice through the spacetime block at various angles, each perceiving a distinct "now." This relativity of simultaneity means that what we consider "the present" is just one of many presents, with no universal 'now' to anchor us.

Yet, this particular outlook is deterministic since the past, present, and future would coexist, clashing with our sense of free will and the unpredictability introduced by quantum mechanics. Quantum randomness suggests that the future cannot be precisely predetermined — that the universe is not deterministic. This inherent uncertainty challenges the notion of an entirely predestined universe, hinting at a more complex interplay between time and the individuals experiencing its subjective flow.

To reconcile these perspectives, one might envision a universe where the block of time is not complete but grows with each new event, weaving together the countless 'nows' experienced by individuals across the cosmos. In this ever-increasing block model, the future remains open to the unfolding of events, thus restoring the possibility of possibility, so to speak. Now, there's a limit to what this ever-increasing block of time could look like, and it's not block-shaped at all but looks like a cone or an hourglass (if we bring the concept of "possible pasts" into the picture).

A "Cone of Time" represents the possible paths that light and signals can take through spacetime emanating from a specific event. Imagine this event as a point in spacetime where the light cone is a three-dimensional model that shows all possible directions light could travel from that event, forming a cone shape.

The future light cone encompasses all possible locations that light could theoretically reach from the event, defining the boundary of causally connected events that could be influenced by the initial one. Conversely, the past light cone includes all points in spacetime from which light could have traveled to reach the event, representing all past moments that could have influenced it. Outside these cones lies the "elsewhere" region, where events are too far apart to have any causal connection due to the finite speed of light. So, from an observer's subjective perspective, the ever-increasing block model could only play out within the cone of time starting from this observer's "now."

Now, what exactly do we mean by "now?" From a physics perspective, "now" refers to a specific point in spacetime, but to us individual human actors, "now" is a prolonged period during which we carry out a particular action. According to Mises, an actor feels uneasy, imagines a state of the world where he has used some means to reach a specific end he assumes will reduce his uneasiness, and acts purposefully — with intent. To further explore the difference between an objective and a subjective "now," let's do a final dive into the weird realm of quantum mechanics.

Quantum entanglement is a phenomenon where particles become interconnected so that one particle's state instantly correlates with the state of another, no matter how far apart they happen to be. This connection is instantaneous, even over vast distances, leading Einstein to famously refer to it as "spooky action at a distance." Although entanglement is commonly discussed in the context of space, extending this concept to time opens intriguing possibilities.

One way that quantum particles relate across time is through the concept of retrocausality. This idea suggests that an event occurring in the future can influence or determine the outcome of an event in the past, which is less far-fetched than it sounds because of the indeterminate nature of quantum states until they are observed.

Experiments involving "delayed-choice" setups and "quantum erasers" hint at this retrocausal influence. In these experiments, decisions made at the time of measurement can seemingly determine the state or properties of particles in the past. This suggests that future choices influence how particles are related or entangled before the choice is made.

Just as quantum states can evolve forward in time, influencing future states, research suggests they can also evolve backward, allowing future states to affect the past! The measurement of a particle's state at one time could be entangled with the state of another particle at a different time, suggesting a form of temporal connection that transcends our usual understanding of cause and effect. If this is the case, there might be such a thing as free will after all.

Whether time is a fixed block, a growing continuum, or something entirely different, its true essence eludes us and will continue to do so during our journeys through it. The nature of time remains a mystery, sitting at the intersection of physics, philosophy, and human experience. Put another way, it intersects systemic academic research, deductive reasoning, and bro-science.

Let's return to our favorite subject for a bit. An intriguing aspect of the Bitcoin timechain is that its time-space (blockspace) comes into existence in blocks as we agree on a certain probabilistic truth. This, in turn, reflects our deepest understanding of the fabric of reality itself and the perceived relationship between the subjective and the objective. Therefore, Bitcoin is a metaphorical anchor to time itself. Time is money. Bitcoin is time.

Regardless of our understanding (or lack thereof) of quantum mechanics, our attention also shapes our realities in pretty straightforward Newtonian ways. Whether we're aware of it or not, our actions influence others and mold the world around us. Even minor actions ripple through society, affecting and changing reality, often called "The Butterfly Effect." The interconnectedness of actions and perceptions underscores the impact each individual can have on the collective human experience. Our focus and attention become the world we live in.

If you're in a crowded room with a murmur and a buzz, and suddenly, someone calls your name, you'll immediately switch your attention to that particular voice. Your name could even be whispered, and you'd still hear it. Where once there was only white noise, now there's a clear signal. Someone is talking to you, and that conversation is your reality now.

Try to recall some of the best moments of your life. Do you think your memories paint an accurate picture of what actually happened or how you truly felt during those moments? Probably not. But it doesn't matter. Your brain evolved to remember the positives and forget the negatives for a good reason.

Almost all successful peoples' autobiographies and other self-improvement books stress the importance of focus, discipline, and optimistic thoughts. No winner ever viewed themselves as the victim during their careers. Life is complicated, and comparing our own struggles with the struggles of others seldom leads anywhere positive.

Remembering life's struggles accurately could turn the most joyful human into the worst Debbie Downer you have ever met. Turn optimism into a defensive weapon, and you'll win the battle of life. Learn to enjoy every moment because it is truly all you have. They're happy, I'm happy. They're not happy? I'm happy. This is the way.

The fact that being optimistic has a positive effect on your life is self-explanatory, but the impact is far more significant than you can imagine. Let's rephrase that — the extent of your imagination might be the only thing hindering you from drastically changing your life. The map you choose to draw influences your territory much more than you might think. You can meme yourself into being. You can live the meme by becoming the dream.

If you focus on being valuable to others, that is what you'll become. If you're valuable to others, they'll be willing to give up things they deem valuable in exchange for your time and efforts. Contrary to what a famous Guinness beer commercial once proclaimed, good things do *not* come to those who wait. Good things come to those who work their asses off to provide others with good things.

The more attention you pay to Clown World, the more it becomes your reality. The only way to make Clown World go away, figuratively and literally, is to focus on something else. Whenever you engage with a clown or a clownish idea, you give them the attention they crave, above all else. You become their amplifier. If you instead ignore them and start building the world you want to live in, you amplify that reality and reduce the clowns' power.

It doesn't matter what idea the clowns are trying to sell — multiple genders, border walls, or jpegs on the blockchain — the best way to stop them is to build something better. As George Bernard Shaw counseled: "Never wrestle with pigs. You both get dirty, and the pig likes it."

Bitcoin Fixes This

Here's a simple question: If you practice doing something, will you become better at doing it? The answer is obvious. It's one of the simplest truths we learn from childhood: practice makes perfect. The more we repeat an activity, the better we become at it, and it doesn't even matter what that thing is. Here's a less obvious follow-up question: Why aren't prices falling?

On the free market, prices fall to their marginal production costs because humans get better at doing stuff over time. So, if practice leads to greater efficiency, then why don't prices of goods and services fall over time? The answer, as bitcoiners have tirelessly pointed out, is that something is fundamentally broken with the money we use.

The obviousness of the insight that all prices ought to decrease over time in a functioning monetary system makes the concept even harder for people to understand. It's almost too simple. The whole point of the free market is the pricing signal — communicating people's wants, needs, and abilities so that everyone can benefit from everyone else's perpetually improving skills.

Money, as has been discussed, has three basic functions: store of value, medium of exchange, and unit of account. Before Bitcoin, absolute scarcity in a medium of exchange wasn't possible. No human has ever experienced living with a finite form of money, let alone a wholly divisible and teleportable one. Under the gold standard, gold miners got better at mining gold at about the same rate as the rest of the world got better at everything else. So the increase in new gold quite accurately reflected the increased productivity of the market. In other words, prices stayed more or less stable over time. Meanwhile, in fiat land, the cost of producing a new dollar is less than that of typing the word "dollar" on a keyboard. Prices denominated in fiat currencies increase over time despite the enormous increases in efficiency everywhere, especially since the arrival of the Internet.

Unlike both gold and fiat, Bitcoin is a different beast altogether. The production of new satoshis is not dependent on the efficiency of Bitcoin miners because the difficulty adjustment algorithm makes Bitcoins harder to mine based on how long it *ought* to take to find them. An ought that was pre-determined and set in stone by Satoshi Nakamoto in 2009.

Humanity has never experienced a medium of exchange with a finite supply let alone one that can be sent seamlessly across space and time. Imagining a world where practically everything can be divided by twenty-one million is almost impossible. Fiat currencies are cheap to produce and, therefore, only capable of half of money's intended functionality — sending value across space. Gold has the opposite problem. It is not easily used for transactions across space, but retains its value over time. Never before has there been a type of money that can do both.

Further, when money lacks the "store of value" functionality, other commodities absorb an economy's monetary premium and become store of value substitutes. Real estate, stocks, and bonds have slowly but surely replaced savings accounts since the dollar lost its last connection to gold in 1971. Post hyperbitcoinization, this tactic will fail. Denominated in Bitcoin, the value of houses, stocks, and other piggy bank replacements will decrease in value over time as they will always be less scarce than satoshis. Powerful deflationary forces become even more evident during the vortex-like transition to a Bitcoin standard we currently live in. When the value of a Bitcoin fluctuates, and the upside price swings are increasing substantially, the value pressure on other assets spirals downward. Outperforming Bitcoin in purchasing power during the upcoming decades will likely prove futile.

Now, what does all this imply? First, we need to examine the concept of deflation itself. We can draw some first-principles conclusions by thinking about deflation in a logically deductive manner. Deflation (usually defined as a general decline in prices) often triggers fear among fiat economists, policymakers, and consumers for several, more or less misinformed, reasons.

Fiat experts erroneously presume that consumers, hoping for better deals, will delay purchases anticipating better deals later. Their concern is that this decrease in spending slows economic growth, as consumption drives a significant portion of economic activity. Another argument is that deflation increases the actual value of debt, making it more expensive for borrowers to repay their loans. Ultimately, the fiat advocates believe this will lead to higher default rates and stress on the banking system.

In reality, however, deflation is a natural market mechanism that corrects investment and consumption imbalances. Similarly, prices adjust to reflect true consumer preferences and resource availability, leading to a more efficient allocation of resources. While it's true that deflation increases the real burden of debt, it is simultaneously true that it incentivizes more prudent borrowing and lending practices. Credit aligns with savings, reducing the likelihood of speculative bubbles fueled by excessive and cheap loans.

The core problem with inflationary currencies is unnaturally cheap loans, which solely exist because people believe in free lunches. Negative interest rates, for instance, contradict the natural human inclination to prefer present consumption over future consumption. An interest rate is the price of the future in terms of the present, which is always more expensive than the future since no human being has a negative time preference. We prefer immediate consumption to delayed consumption. Negative interest rates, therefore, are not genuinely negative but are a facade, as they're always accompanied by an increased money supply, leading to inflation. Governments and central banks inject money into the economy, artificially lowering interest rates to stimulate spending, which devalues currency over time, meaning savers and investors effectively pay for negative rates through reduced purchasing power.

Eager to dodge blame for the inevitable pain that accompanies rebooting a crumbling financial system, politicians gleefully roll the inflationary snowball further and further down the hill. But the economic reboot must happen. Boom-bust cycles, hyperinflation, and depressions are all symptoms of the underlying cancer — inflationary money. When central banks artificially lower interest rates, they encourage excessive borrowing and investment, leading to an unsustainable boom. Eventually, the misallocation of resources becomes evident, causing a bust as everyone starts selling off all their overvalued stuff. Characterized by high unemployment, low output, and deflation or severe inflation based on monetary policy responses, depressions are severe, prolonged economic downturns following economic busts. Only markets correcting themselves without government intervention can restore economic balance. Inflation is, therefore, simply hyperinflation in slow motion. Since no politician or central banker has any incentive to let the bust happen naturally, the inflationary snowball perpetually picks up speed, eventually causing prices to rise in a hockey-stick-curve-like fashion.

Deflation alarmists claim that as prices fall, companies may see their revenues decline without a corresponding decrease in costs, squeezing profits. Lower profits lead to reduced investment in capital and research, further hampering economic growth. However, deflation resulting from productivity gains (such as technological innovation) is, by definition, beneficial. Lower prices benefit everyone. They reflect an increase in goods and services, meaning that society is wealthier overall. Adaptive and innovative businesses can survive and thrive in a deflationary environment if they focus on long-term, sustainable investments rather than short-term gains.

Jevons' Paradox, named after British economist William Stanley Jevons, who observed his effect in the 19th century with coal consumption, is an economic concept that describes a counterintuitive situation in which increases in the efficiency of resource use lead to higher (rather than lower) overall consumption of that resource. Higher overall consumption occurs because efficiency gains decrease the cost per unit, making the resource more attractive and affordable for a broader range of uses. As a result, the total demand for the resource increases, often outstripping the initial savings achieved through efficiency gains.

Jevons' Paradox also occurs during periods of sound money, even when the overall price level in an economy is falling. In other words, efficiency improvements still make specific resources cheaper in deflationary times. The increased efficiency spurs greater consumption because the relative affordability encourages additional uses. Hence, despite the broader economic trend of falling prices and less consumption, the targeted resource sees a rise in demand, illustrating Jevons' Paradox. The deflationary nature of data storage is a nice example, as more disk space is sold every year despite each terabyte continuously dropping in price, even when adjusted for inflation.

Wages and prices are flexible. In a deflationary environment, wages will adjust to reflect changing economic conditions, stabilizing employment without inflationary policies. The Keynesian emphasis on nominal wage rigidity as a justification for inflation to reduce unemployment is fear-mongering. These kinds of Keynesian theories are popular among statists because they serve as excuses for the men behind the curtain to let their money printers run amok and sneakily make every citizen work for them instead of for themselves.

An economy with a fixed money supply is a different thing — a very different thing. For most of human history, prices have stayed relatively stable compared to what's to come. As discussed, the ability to find new gold and dig it out of the ground has advanced in tandem with other technological advancements, making prices denominated in gold relatively stable across the centuries. Since the abandonment of the gold standard, rapid technological advancements have held consumer prices relatively stable despite enormous drops in actual production and transportation costs. After the emergence of the Internet in general, and smartphones in particular, coordinating workers and supply chains worldwide has become almost trivial compared to the relative nightmare it presented even a couple of decades ago.

With money tethered only to its own printer, inflation has moved the world's wealth from the monetary medium into luxury assets. The cost of fine art, Lamborghinis, and metropolitan real estate has risen much faster than breakfast cereal, teddy bears, or duct tape. Most bitcoiners understand that this effectively funnels wealth from the poor to the rich. But what's harder to imagine is what a reversal of the process would look like. Is there a future in which Manhattan apartments lose value over time? The answer is that you're already living in this future if you're using the correct denominator!

You have to start measuring value with the correct unit to get a glimpse of this already present future. As a medium of exchange, money does not contain inherent value but facilitates the exchange of goods and services to which individuals subjectively attach value. Therefore, money cannot really be a yardstick of value since it cannot quantify an individual's satisfaction or perceived utility from a good or service. Here, it is essential to highlight the role of prices as signals as they convey information about the relative scarcity and preferences for available goods and services. Money facilitates these prices, but the information content lies in the price ratios themselves, not in the monetary unit. As an aside, Bitcoin is more akin to a yardstick than other forms of money because it is nothing more than information. The satoshis don't exist in physical reality or even digitally since all that's on the ledger is unspent transaction outputs. The satoshis are all in your head, which is a feature — not a bug. So, since money can never really be an objective measurement tool due to the subjective nature of human value judgments, the term "store of value" is flawed. Saving is simply trading with your future self. Therefore, the term "medium of exchange over time" is more accurate.

Mises defined money as "the most marketable commodity." He also wrote (in *Human Action*) that "Money is nothing but a medium of exchange, and it completely fulfills its function when the exchange of goods and services is carried on more easily with its help than would be possible to means of barter." You might have heard people argue about which of the core functions of money (store of value, medium of exchange, and unit of account) is most important. From the "medium of exchange applies to both time and space" perspective, the temporal function must necessarily precede the spatial one since no exchange happens outside of time. In layman's terms, money must hold its value over time before acquiring any other function. Thus, medium of exchange over *time* supersedes medium of exchange over *space*. From a money-printing entity's perspective, the temporal aspect is entirely redundant since the entity's goal is to counterfeit and spend as much as possible while it still can.

Governments create economic inefficiencies by prioritizing wealth distribution and central planning over personal freedoms. And yes, central banking is central planning! When you mess with incentives and the pricing mechanism of the free market, resources get misallocated, and shortages inevitably follow. Without a profit motive, people's incentives for innovation and productivity gradually disappear. Distorting the market signals with interventionist policies deprives producers of their only tool for assessing what to produce and in what quantities — you guessed it, the price signal!

Moreover, the administration of an interventionist economy requires extensive bureaucracy. Expanding governmental control spawns inefficiencies and a cumbersome regulatory environment, disincentivizing individual initiatives and entrepreneurship. Bullshit, dear reader, is everywhere. The bureaucracy eventually becomes so convoluted that it hinders the very objectives it was meant to achieve, such as improving welfare or streamlining distribution. As Oscar Wilde put it: "The bureaucracy is expanding to meet the needs of the expanding bureaucracy."

If a politician's goal is equity and community ownership, infringements on people's freedoms and individual rights are unavoidable. Efforts to enforce equality result in a lack of recognition for individual effort and achievement, demotivating individuals from striving for excellence and leading to a cultural atmosphere where mediocrity is encouraged. All redistribution schemes are costly affairs. They do not fall to their marginal cost of production since governments compete in producing "bads" rather than goods. On the contrary, redistribution becomes more costly over time, and its effects are not easily reversed. If you punish excellence and encourage mediocrity, mediocrity is what you'll get. You cannot achieve equality without sacrificing quality.

Assessing what value someone or something ought to have on the market becomes much easier when each individual has an incorruptible number against which to measure their lives. You merely have to observe Bitcoin's purchasing power over time. How many iPhones will one Bitcoin buy today, and how many could it buy ten years ago? How many cars? Mansions? Wives? What should be evident to everyone is that, despite its volatility, the purchasing power of a Bitcoin increases over time.

The easiest way to get a grip on a trend in Bitcoin's price is, as always, to disregard as much noise as possible. Ignore the peaks, primarily driven by a "fear of missing out" and professional traders taking advantage of psychological phenomena in weaker minds. Look instead to the yearly lows, where you'll see a steady rise and an average increase of around 200% per year since inception. Every price is at the crosshairs of where supply meets demand, and Bitcoin is the only asset in the world with a mathematically fixed supply.

Since there's no example of anything remotely similar to Bitcoin in history, no one knows how a finite asset will behave on the market. What we do know is how the opposite behaves. Fiat currencies ensure that prices increase over time, giving everyone on Earth, individuals and companies alike, an incentive to spend rather than save. Where inflation is higher, the incentive is stronger. Bitcoin stands as the literal inverse of the current system.

In mathematics, an inverse is essentially the opposite of something. Inversing allows you to "undo" or reverse the effects of the original operation/function. Imagine a simple action like walking ten steps backward. The inverse of this action would be walking ten steps forward, bringing you right back to where you started. If you multiply a number by twenty-one, the inverse operation would be dividing it by twenty-one, reversing the original multiplication. Usually, when we talk about an inverse, we talk about it in this sense: one divided by something else. The more of this something we put in the denominator, the less of this something we get as a result.

Bitcoin inverses all the incentives that lead to Clown World. In other words, you can reverse the Clown World degeneration process by adopting Bitcoin. Unlike fiat's ever-expanding supply, Bitcoin's never-expanding supply incentivizes its users to save rather than spend. It shifts society's political power from those closest to the money printer to those most productive. Success in the Bitcoin world comes from providing value to your fellow human beings, not mass theft or political manipulation. Everything Divided by 21 Million equals the inverse of Clown World.

Freedom Footprint

The left isn't right, and there's no right left, right?

In political philosophy, a fundamental divide exists between positive and negative human rights. Positive rights are entitlements that require other humans to provide goods or services, often dictated by the government. In other words, someone must do something to fulfill someone else's positive right. A right to free healthcare, education, or Universal Basic Income is always inextricably linked to someone else's duty to obey orders.

In stark contrast, negative rights act as the guardians of individual liberty. They demand not action but inaction—freedom from interference, a sanctuary from violations against material and physical property. When we speak of negative rights, we invoke the hallowed principles of free speech, privacy, and freedom from torture. Negative rights are not guarantees of what we shall receive but solemn vows of what must remain untouched.

To the logical mind, these definitions invariably lead to one fundamental question: Can a positive right even exist without violating a negative one? Try to devise a situation where this is the case! From a first-principles standpoint, there can only be one true human right since there's only one right that can be universally true for every human being that has ever lived and that ever will — the right to be left alone.

If the right to be left alone is violated, regardless of whether the violation is carried out by a government or any other criminal organization, all you have left is the right to obey. This is the core tenet of the non-aggression principle in libertarian philosophy: No human has any right to force their will onto another.

Property rights lie at the heart of all rights, including free speech. The right to express oneself freely is inherently tied to the ownership and control of property. Significantly, property rights are not merely about owning physical goods or land but also encompass control over one's body and the fruits of one's labor. In this context, free speech is a property right because expressing oneself is an exercise in control over one's body and thoughts. Therefore, the protection of property rights inherently includes the protection of the freedom to speak.

In *The Ethics of Liberty*, Murray Rothbard astutely noted that the loudest proponents of freedom of speech often leave out a crucial question: *where* should people be "allowed" to exercise this "right" to express themselves? The answer is simple — on their property. You decide who gets to say what in your house. *You* dictate the rules of *your* social media platform. Property rights maximalism is the correct "lawful" stance.

From this viewpoint, freedom of speech is naturally limited by the boundaries of one's property. From a lawfulness perspective, individuals can speak freely within their own property or on any platform where the property owner consents to their speech, respecting the autonomy of the individual property owner and upholding the principle of consent as central to exercising any rights within a society. The key point here is that one's right to free speech does not extend to the property of others without their consent. To impose upon a property owner the obligation to host or permit speech they disagree with or find objectionable infringes upon their property rights. Such an imposition negates the principle of consent and undermines the foundation of individual liberty. So-called "public property" can only exist if preceded by expropriation and property rights violations, including "public service" media outlets and state-subsidized newspapers.

Moreover, any state intervention that compels speech or prohibits certain expressions on private property infringes on the owner's property rights. If a state should exist at all, which is debatable, that state's role should be limited to protecting life, liberty, and property, thereby ensuring freedom of speech by protecting the rights of property owners to control their domain. Sadly, this is seldom the case.

Ridding yourself of as many forceful interactions as possible isn't exclusively beneficial to you but to everyone around you. Entities monopolizing violence in a specific geographical area tend to fund themselves by forcefully extracting wealth from everyone living there. This is true for governments, cartels, mafias, criminal gangs, and all other violent institutions.

The larger the criminal entity, the more it will try to legitimize its existence through propaganda, claiming to "protect" you from some evil, usually from theft or other violations of your "human rights." But if the only true human right is the right to be left alone, how could protection ever be involuntary? They're the ones stealing your stuff. They're the ones telling your kids how to live. They're the ones lying about your rights. You're the carbon they wish to reduce, the junkie they wish to imprison, and the terrorist they want you to fear. The only tangible difference between a government and a Mexican drug cartel is that at least the cartel doesn't force you to take their drugs and pay for them, too.

If you don't care whether you provide value to others, the safest route to achieve success in Clown World is to go down the government-approved path of university studies. If you do, you'll get to put some letters after your name on LinkedIn. After that, you might end up at a company that actually does stuff, but there's a high risk that you'll end up in the so-called public sector or start working for a lubrication company. A lubrication company's sole purpose is to offer companies that actually do things a little protection from the government. Accounting firms, tax lawyers, and other professional services companies are basically just lube salesmen whose products all have the same single purpose — to make the giant government dildo hurt a little less when it inevitably arrives to rape you.

The fight for freedom is neverending; every generation must participate or be forever shackled to its hamster's wheels. The siren's song of the government has led many adventurers to live in a state of perpetual Stockholm Syndrome. Even though the beaches are littered with human skulls, her song seduces new sailors daily: "Free health care! Universal Basic Income! Fix the weather! Free lunches abound!"

Akin to when a diabetic forgets their insulin shot, the government's anaconda grip over your life tightens every time another freedom is sacrificed on the altar of perceived safety. She is a cunning snake that grows stronger whenever we forget to resist. The history of human civilization is one of repeating cycles over the centuries — property rights lead to prosperity, prosperity leads to more government spending, more government spending leads to bigger government, bigger government leads to delusions of grandeur and totalitarianism, and totalitarianism leads to civil wars and revolutions.

Are you prepared to take matters into your own hands? Probably not. You still live in the world you were born into, and idealistic martyrdom is not on most people's bucket lists. But whatever small step you take to increase your personal freedom footprint increases the total level of freedom dioxide in the atmosphere. Freedom dioxide is essential to life. It prevents political climate change and global laming.

Adopting Bitcoin helps you emit more freedom dioxide than anything else. The rabbit hole is bottomless, and you can be a bitcoiner to whatever extent you want. From taking your coins off an exchange to getting a hardware wallet to running a node to coinjoining to setting up multi-sig to mining to working for a Bitcoin company to contributing to Bitcoin's codebase — all of these require different levels of commitment and conviction. The typical bitcoiner path is to buy some, watch in awe as it appreciates, think "holy shit! I've got to secure my coins," and then most of the other steps eventually follow.

An important rite of passage for every bitcoiner is running a node. You don't absolutely have to run a node, but if you don't, you rely on third parties to verify and honestly report on the state of the Bitcoin network. Running a node is not trivial, but it is not insurmountably difficult either. Just get a dedicated computer for your node, make sure it's not contaminated with viruses and malware, and download your preferred Bitcoin client. You can even use a plug-and-play node-in-a-box solution if you so choose. Connect to the Internet, download the timechain, and voila! You're running Bitcoin.

Node decentralization ensures that Bitcoin cannot be arbitrarily controlled or manipulated by any single entity, preserving its integrity and trustworthiness. However, these characteristics are under constant threat, and if lost, Bitcoin risks devolving into just another shitcoin, indistinguishable from anything else in the ever-growing pile of cryptographic fecal matter.

Unfortunately, at the time of writing, the cost of running a Bitcoin node has started to rise significantly. Specifically, the initial block download has become more burdensome to the computer because arbitrary data has been increasingly clogging the timechain recently. Older and more inexpensive hardware can no longer download and sync the blocks in a reasonable amount of time. In other words, the cost of firing up a node is rising. Bitcoin only works because anyone can run a node. Keeping Bitcoin node operation costs low is more crucial for Bitcoin's survival than maintaining low transaction fees. While both costs will likely rise over time, affordable node operation is more critical for the network.

Regardless of whether you're running a node, you should take proper self-custody of your coins. Recall the difference between ownership and possession and how there's no difference between ownership, possession, and knowledge when it comes to Bitcoin. Bitcoins held by a custodian are in the physical control of that custodian and, therefore, not "yours" in any true sense of the word. You *must* take your coins off the exchange and put them into self-custody to own them *at all*.

Besides the hodlers and the noderunners, miners play a crucial role in securing the Bitcoin network. However, they do not, *and should not*, have the power to dictate its rules. Miners don't "make" or "find" bitcoins. They find *valid blocks* and get paid by the network (in satoshis) for doing so. The balance of power within the Bitcoin ecosystem is delicate, and decisions about the network's future should be made by all of its users, not just a small group of mining pool owners. You can't really call yourself a Bitcoin miner if all you're doing is selling computing power to a non-transparent pool. Since solo mining is almost entirely futile at this point, your only option to mine in a self-sovereign way is to select a pool where you can verify how your computing power is actually being used (or, better yet, one that lets you construct your own blocks).

Bitcoins can be used in many ways, and nothing stops you from using different parts of your stack for different things. If you've acquired your bitcoins on an exchange with a KYC policy, they're most likely tracked by some chain analytics company. These companies pretend to know who owns what in Bitcoin and then sell that data to exchanges and institutions. The exchanges need the data as governments often force them to extract as much information as possible about their customers. The fact that you can't really prove who owns a Bitcoin doesn't matter to these people. All they crave is "plausible connectivity," which they claim proves ownership. It doesn't.

Most chain analytics companies (henceforth called chain-anal companies) display their data similarly. A user's coins are given a risk score based on behavior heuristics and how many "risky addresses" your coins are associated with. If any of your coins are in any way connected to an address used for buying drugs, money laundering, or assumed to be controlled by ISIS (or equally evil Canadian truck-driving terrorists), the software flags the addresses and assigns them a higher risk score. If the risk score exceeds a certain threshold, some exchanges freeze your funds, and others even notify local authorities. Do not trust KYC Bitcoin exchanges!

Coinjoined transactions also receive a risk score if detected by the chain-anal software. A Coinjoin is a multi-party Bitcoin transaction in which all parties put in and get out a certain amount of Bitcoin, but the addresses are mixed in the transaction, making the coins' origin virtually impossible to trace. There are plenty of reasons to increase your privacy by coinjoining. One is to break the links between the transactions that came before your UTXO, allowing you to save or spend your satoshis as you see fit without the risk of being tracked by the watchful panoptic eye of Sauron and his chain-anal orcs. Another reason is that your participation in the coinjoin increases the privacy of every other Bitcoin user. The more obfuscated the overall UTXO history, the harder it becomes for authorities and other bad actors to prove anything by "tracking coins" in the future.

The risk score the chain-anal software attaches to your conjoin transaction depends on the transactions with which you happen to join yours. For example, if you join your coins with coins from an address associated with ISIS (or Gord, the Canadian trucker), your coinjoined UTXO will receive a higher risk score.

Some coinjoining coordinators use the chain-anal companies' "black lists" against themselves by not allowing blacklisted UTXOs to coinjoin at all. In doing so, they ensure that the coinjoin itself is not given a higher risk score by the chain-anal software. In other words, it helps the end user stay below the radar.

We will have to tolerate all of this chain-anal nonsense during Bitcoin's adoption phase since most governments still don't understand that money is speech. As time passes, it will be harder to prove the origin of specific coins as they will eventually get mixed up with other coins in one way or another. For now, coinjoins are a great tool to increase your financial privacy.

Many tools will help you achieve greater freedom. Bitcoin is the most obvious one, but others are vastly underappreciated. Video conferencing, for instance. Nowadays, virtually everyone can look each other in the eye and communicate verbally without lag, no matter how geographically far apart they are. Combine that with Bitcoin, and you quickly realize that national borders are already obsolete. If no one can stop you from communicating, not even monetarily, barriers to global commerce dissolve. "If goods and services don't cross borders, soldiers will," the saying goes, and right now, it's way easier for a service than a soldier to cross a national border.

Apart from your online connections, getting to know bitcoiners away from your keyboard is not only a pleasant and rewarding thing to do but an insurance policy against the collapse of your local government kleptocurrency. Connecting with fellow bitcoin maximalists is a remarkable experience. Whether in person or online, these encounters allow you to bypass all formalities and skip the superficial small talk about the weather. You immediately know the person you're engaging with has surpassed several cognitive and ethical thresholds. Since we are our satoshis, we all have several incentives to be as friendly and helpful to one another as possible. What is good for the individual bitcoiner is also good for Bitcoin, and vice versa. The Bitcoin community is replete with conferences, meetups, shindigs, orgies, and walks happening regularly in almost every major city in the world (and in many minor ones too). There are also a whole bunch of handy apps for finding other bitcoiners in your area. The deeper into hyperbitcoinization we go, the more powerful these tools become.

Successful apps and websites eventually become honeypots for hackers and itchy-fingered government interventionist bureaucrats. Hacking can mostly be defended against by following good security practices, but protecting your software from the full force of nation-level monopolized violence is another matter. The harsh truth is that almost every human being can be bought or threatened into complying with nearly anything, but as Jeff Goldblum's character said in *Jurassic Park*, "Life finds a way." On the Internet, life finds its way through decentralization. Where there was once BitPay, there's now BTC Pay Server. Where there was Local Bitcoins, there is now a plethora of peer-to-peer exchanges. More freedom tools are born every year, but perhaps the most important addition is a little protocol called Nostr.

Nostr, short for "Notes and Other Stuff Transmitted by Relays," is an innovative protocol designed to create a more open, private, and free-speech-oriented Internet. Unlike traditional social networks that rely on centralized servers controlled by corporations, Nostr operates on a decentralized network of relays. This architecture prevents any single entity from gaining control of the network, as users always have the option to take their stuff to other clients and relays. Since Nostr has no single point of failure or authority, it is much harder for governments or corporations to censor or manipulate content on Nostr platforms.

Having a Nostr profile in parallel with your other social media accounts is highly recommended since doing so provides at least some protection from shadowbanning and other forms of censorship. Although Nostr lacks the first-mover network effects of the traditional platforms, it is proliferating rapidly and has enormous potential. Almost anything can be built on top of the protocol, and most clients have an infrastructure for Bitcoin lightning payments-as-likes, known as "zaps." One way to increase your freedom footprint is to start using Nostr.

In addition to employing freedom tools, there are also things to avoid if your goal is to optimize your freedoms. First, you should know that almost everything marketed as "free" is probably more expensive than you think. Remember — there is no free lunch! If it's free, you're the product. If it's tax-funded, it's not free, *and* you're still the product.

The "if it's free, I'm the product" mindset is essential to preserve your online integrity. This isn't to say that online services are necessarily good just because you pay for them, but please think twice before you upload naked pictures of your kids to a free cloud storage service. The cloud storage options offered by the titans of the Internet may seem safe for now, but they're far from invulnerable. Behind every server password is a human being, and human beings are not immune to threats of violence.

Freedom is all about optionality. Privacy is the ability to selectively reveal parts of your life to others. Some people want to take your stuff and enslave you. Some will succeed. One thing you can do to be more selective regarding what laws you need to obey is to get a second passport.

Flag Theory is one strategy for maximizing personal sovereignty. The theory is premised on diversifying one's lifestyle, assets, and business affairs across multiple countries to reduce risk and increase individual freedom. In a nutshell, it's about being independent of any single country or government.

Jurisdictional arbitrage does require significant resources and is more applicable to high-net-worth individuals than the common pleb. That said, new options are emerging every day for the more modest bitcoiner. Residency-hopping and living as a digital nomad is often easier than fighting state bureaucracy locally. Already a handful of passport/residency/golden visa options are available for purchase around the globe, and when denominated in Bitcoin, the cost of increasing your jurisdictional independence decreases over time.

More and more people are adopting Bitcoin as their primary currency, strengthening the Bitcoin network while weakening the legacy system. As more people take advantage of jurisdictional arbitrage, states become increasingly pressured to adapt to this new reality or risk a severe brain drain. In other words, they are forced to become more Bitcoin-friendly or suffer the consequences. Ironically enough, the more brain drain a nation suffers, the fewer brains there will be around to solve the brain drain problem. Bitcoin nation-state adoption game theory is playing out in real-time.

Tax laws surrounding Bitcoin vary significantly from country to country, reflecting various governments' "diverse" approaches to regulating, taxing, and recognizing it. Most governmental agencies are also yet to recognize the difference between Bitcoin and shitcoins and therefore treat them as if they were the same. El Salvador's contrarian treatment of Bitcoin as the premier currency is the obvious exception. Virtually all other governments demand a cut from Bitcoin's so-called "gains" against their collapsing fiat currencies. Still, tax policies are almost only problematic when selling satoshis for fiat currency in a government-regulated bank account. Peer-to-peer transactions in Bitcoin are practically impossible for any authority to do anything about. Whenever you find yourself surrounded by bitcoiners, you'll quickly notice how nearly all problems surrounding money go away. Usually, at least someone has some fiat to pay for dinners and whatnot, and any bill can always be split using satoshis.

Experiencing the frictionless nature of Bitcoin is genuinely eye-opening and gives you a glimpse into the future. The main obstacles are the off-ramps to the legacy fiat system. A bank is akin to a 2-of-3 multi-sig wallet where you, the bank, and the government hold one key each. In other words, money in the bank is not really yours. Nor is it really money at all. In Bitcoin, every individual is sovereign. When centralized institutions and national borders fade, a company can be something as simple as a chat group.

There's no turning back once you experience the frictionlessness of Bitcoin and start seeing the world as it truly is. The people in power have that power because their populations believe they do. All emperors are naked underneath the facade, and the best way to strip them of their power is to start using as many freedom tools as possible right now. Stop listening to their lies and enabling them by using money they can counterfeit. The bills they print are claims on your stuff. Whenever you accept them, you prolong the scheme. Bitcoin is the sly, roundabout way to introduce something they cannot stop, the answer Friedrich Hayek envisioned all those years ago. Don't fear the future. Embrace it. Increase your freedom footprint.

That Which You Can Do Without

In the closing scenes of the movie *Into The Wild*, the protagonist, Christopher McCandless, confronts the ultimate consequences of his quest for solitude and communion with nature while completely isolated from society. After months of living in the wilds of Alaska in an abandoned bus, McCandless finally succumbs to the harsh realities of wilderness survival when his story tragically ends as he starves to death shortly after being poisoned by toxic plants. Lying on his deathbed in his death bus, McCandless reflects on his life and experiences. He finally realizes the importance of human connections, scrawling "Happiness only real when shared" into his diary. The first prerequisite for any human interaction is someone to interact with.

Bitcoin changes you more than you can change it. Embracing Bitcoin is akin to adopting a more accurate world map. At any point in life, all you can play are the cards you have in your hand at that specific moment. Now, what are those cards? Well, that depends on the cards you were dealt at the start of the game and, more importantly, how well you've played your cards up to this point. The cards you have on hand at the moment represent your currently available means. The better your cards, the more plentiful the ends available, and the quicker you can reach them. Your means cards fall into three categories: capital, skills, and human connections. Bitcoin, as we will explore, ticks all three boxes.

The first category, capital, encompasses your physical possessions and money. Capital refers to goods and resources you employ to produce more complex goods and services. Capital goods include physical assets such as real estate, precious metals, stocks, and money, which can all be used to generate more capital or be traded for other goods and services. Capital structure and temporal coordination between production processes are critical for economic calculation and the efficient allocation of resources over time. Your physical possessions are precious, but their physicality makes them vulnerable to theft, socialism, and natural disasters.

The second category, knowledge, is less sensitive to outside forces. Knowledge is an easy burden to carry. If your goal is optionality, investing in yourself and your skill set is a no-brainer for your brain. There's a high probability that you discovered Bitcoin because of your inquisitive mind, and Bitcoin probably led you down a path of more inquiry. Leveling up your knowledge is an excellent way of increasing your value to others and making them more valuable to you.

The value of other people brings us to the third category of life cards: your network. The people you know, and your relationships with them obviously have a significant impact on your life. One could even go so far as to say they are your life. At the very least, other people are crucial to your long-term survival. Even the most stubborn defenders of uncompromising individualism (such as the authors of this book) have to admit that human beings are flock animals. Surrounding yourself with the right people is paramount to accomplishing a successful life, no matter how you happen to define "success." If you have a day job, your employer and colleagues play a huge role here. If you're an entrepreneur, your customers and clients do. Either way, your reputation and the people you interact with will seriously affect your life.

Bitcoin is all three types of cards at once. It is clearly capital, as you can use it as a medium of exchange and unit of account through time and space. It is also knowledge, as proper Bitcoin usage requires at least *some* level of expertise in multiple fields. Bitcoin indirectly forces you to level up your skills with computers, computer networks, mathematics, and economics, as insufficient proficiency in these areas has the potential to become very costly. Finally, as we've explored, you *are* your satoshis, and so is everyone else who owns some. Exchanging or accepting satoshis for goods and services requires you to interact with at least this part of the person you're trading with — the pseudonymous part.

You cannot "own" Bitcoin in the traditional sense of owning stuff. No matter what governments, courts, chain-anal people, or anyone else tells you, there is no way to prove that someone *doesn't* know a string of information, such as a private key. From this perspective, satoshis are never transferred but merely reorganized on the timechain for communication purposes.

Put another way, the twelve magic words do not belong to anyone. They're just twelve words. At its core, the private key that unlocks an unspent Bitcoin transaction output (UTXO) is nothing but a string of ones and zeroes. The implications of the satoshis residing within our minds are way more significant than any living politician can comprehend. Bitcoin has made it blatantly apparent that money was never anything but information, but what this means is yet to be fully understood.

Any government ban on "self-hosted" or "non-custodial" Bitcoin wallets would be as absurd as a ban on using your brain. Such a ban would have severe consequences. It would deny you the right to keep a secret while granting the government the right to claim that you do and transform everyone from a potential criminal to an actual one. If you cannot prove that you're unaware of the numbers one and zero when such a ban is in place, a court could never rule out that you could own *all* the bitcoins. You would have to prove that you *don't* know something, which is impossible. You would be guilty until proven innocent, which would be something you could never possibly prove. Any law that stops or restricts Bitcoin usage is nothing less than a crime against humanity, and we should all treat it as such.

There's a high likelihood that we'll see more court cases involving bitcoiners in many jurisdictions in the future. The precedents set by these courts will largely determine how difficult life as a bitcoiner will be during the transition to hyperbitcoinization. For those not super keen on buying a one-way ticket to El Salvador, these fights are worth taking on. They are good hills to die on. Orange-pill your local lawmen and politicians as soon as you can!

You may think that laws prohibiting the use of numbers are too absurd to ever come into practice. But the concept of "illegal numbers" already exists. An "illegal number" refers to a specific number subject to legal restrictions, making its "possession," distribution, or use illegal. Illegal numbers represent data that infringes on digital copyright, contains encryption keys, or comprises other sensitive information that authorities deem restricted. The concept of illegal numbers rose to prominence during the DeCSS numbers case in the early 2000s. The case centered around the distribution of a small piece of code called DeCSS, which could decrypt the copy protection (Content Scramble Systems) on DVDs. The case gained widespread attention when cypherpunks repeatedly published the DeCSS code as a series of prime numbers on Digg, a popular social media site. Arguing that numbers themselves couldn't be copyrighted, prime number activists also posted a picture called the "Free Speech Flag," a hexadecimal color representation of said encryption key, in defiance of censorship efforts.

The notion of illegal numbers is just as weird as it sounds. But laws that could jail you for uttering a number in certain jurisdictions do, in fact, exist. In examining how such extreme laws come into being, we must go back to reasoning from first principles and remember the difference between "legal" and "lawful." From a first principles property rights maximalist perspective, copyright laws are all bullshit because the concept of "intellectual property" makes no sense.

Property, defined as the exclusive right to use, control, or dispose of tangible (or intangible) assets, is fundamentally about the relationship between an individual and an item. The concept of property should serve as a bridge between subjective valuations and objective reality, *not* the relationship between people and information. Sadly, this is hardly the case anywhere.

Applied to scarce resources, property rights reduce conflict over physical goods. Intellectual property, however, involves ideas and information which are inherently non-scarce and non-rivalrous. Unlike physical property, ideas can be shared and used by all people simultaneously without depletion. Thus, enforcing exclusive rights over ideas contradicts the natural characteristic of information and knowledge as infinitely replicable.

Intellectual property laws interfere with price signals and other mechanisms of the free market and make it more challenging to allocate resources efficiently, which distorts the market's ability to determine the most valued use of physical resources. By granting exclusive rights to creators and patent owners, intellectual property laws inhibit others from improving upon or competing with the protected ideas, slowing innovation. To put it bluntly, intellectual property laws literally retard the entire market.

Even if you do believe in copyright laws and things like illegal numbers, you'll have to admit that a law requiring a person to prove that they DON'T know a particular number is absurd. But this is what a ban on owning Bitcoin would have to be. Such laws are already in place, such as the Digital Millennium Copyright Act (DMCA) which you've no doubt come across when searching the web to obtain movies or music. When contemplating the implications of this sort of thing, a specific question inevitably arises: "How unjust of a society am I willing to live in?". What are you willing to put up with, and what would the consequences be if you didn't?

Disobeying the law can have severe consequences, but blind obedience is even worse. We are facing a societal paradigm shift of immense proportions, where our perseverance in the present will determine the fate of our children's future. Are you willing to stand your ground and fight for your freedoms, or will you choose the convenience of being mere voting cattle? Are you willing to bite the hand that allegedly feeds you?

Most of us don't want to be martyrs. We are content as long as we have a roof over our heads and three daily meals to look forward to. But being content is what enables the zookeepers to keep you caged. Where is your line in the sand? How many freedoms are you willing to toss on the altar of comfort? How slippery is the slope to totalitarianism?

Since Bitcoin is all about truth and no authority figure can tell you what Bitcoin should mean to *you*, reputational capital is arguably more critical among bitcoiners than in any other community. No other community is so relentless when calling out dishonest or immoral behavior. The unforgiving, uncompromising nature of the so-called "toxic maxis" is a feature rather than a bug and an essential part of Bitcoin's immune system. Ultimately, we all become more robust because of the refusal to blindly follow self-proclaimed leaders.

Bitcoin erases the boundary between property rights and free speech. It illuminates that the two are inseparable, as there's no difference between knowledge and ownership in Bitcoin. The right to freely express oneself has to play second fiddle to property rights, as infringements of the latter are impossible without wing-clipping the former. Put another way, freedom of expression without property rights is little more than the right to openly complain when one's possessions are being "legally" expropriated. Actions speak louder than words, and the fact that some people voluntarily move from freedom-of-speech-oriented Western democracies to property-rights-upholding monarchies such as Dubai and Thailand reveals what they value the most.

Expressing yourself through action reveals the real you. Without the unadulterated ability to do so, you have no choice but to live your life as something other than your honest self. Since taxes and inflation are everywhere, it is fair to say that being your authentic self is not affordable for almost any human being living today. Not even the super-rich can be true to themselves, as they are not immune to the personality changes that come with the ever-decreasing purchasing power of society's primary exchange medium. Deceitful thieves thrive in societies built from a base layer of theft and deceit.

A monetary base layer built on absolute truth would create the opposite scenario. A world so much better that the human mind can't comprehend what it would look like. The fiat mind can't understand deflation as a positive. If you still think about Bitcoin's purchasing power in fiat terms, you're missing the point. The dollar is nearly useless as a measuring tool for intersubjective value statements, and measuring the price of a Bitcoin in dollar terms furthers the confusion inherent in the oppressive legacy system we're trying to escape. Not only does the dollar lose value over time, but its inflation warps the market's ability to reduce all prices to their marginal cost of production. The Cantillon Effect and the resource misallocation that inevitably flows from it distort the market signal, making cheap things expensive and expensive things cheap.

One example of Cantillon Effect over-pricing is the infamous *Comedian*, an art piece created by Italian artist Maurizio Cattelan. First displayed at Art Basel in Miami Beach in 2019, the piece, consisting of a single banana duct-taped to a wall, sold for an astonishing $120,000. In true modern art form, the buyer did not even acquire the physical banana but an "art certificate" proving ownership. The owner was instructed to replace the banana when it eventually decayed, and doing so would ensure the piece would still be considered an authentic Cattelan artwork. Only in a world where money is cheaper to produce than everything else do prices go bananas to the point where banana art certificates become worth more than the bananas themselves.

Unfortunately, easily duplicatable nonsense posing as art has also become a thing in Bitcoin. As Bitcoin matures and adoption proliferates, straight-up shitcoin scams become more challenging to pull off. Therefore, scammers have been forced to reinvent themselves, and one such reinvention is the introduction of "ordinal theory" in early 2023. A cunning group of charlatans semi-successfully fooled nocoiners, "crypto" people, and other misguided newbies into believing that satoshis can be arranged ordinally and, therefore, considered "rare." Since the satoshi is nothing but a measuring unit, the notion of a "rare" satoshi is as absurd as a "rare centimeter."

Still, these people somehow manage to sell pictures of monkeys and various "tokens" by clogging Bitcoin transaction data with arbitrary nonsense while claiming that doing so "proves" something about the data. The satoshi is valuable because it is scarce and lives in your head, which cannot be said about any other data on the timechain. Buying a token or a picture on the timechain is even more absurd than buying an "I have the right to duct tape a banana to the wall and call it art" -certificate since it's more akin to purchasing a star in the Andromeda galaxy. It's there, sure, but you can't do anything with it, and everyone else can see it just as much as you can. The difference is that these "ordinals," "inscriptions," and "runes" are not in another galaxy but involuntarily stored on people's nodes right here on Earth.

The ability of regular people to run nodes is crucial for Bitcoin's survival. Every self-reflecting bitcoiner should prioritize doing their part in keeping the timechain as devoid of unnecessary nonsense as possible. Whether you do this by running a node, mining with a transparent pool, or educating people about what makes Bitcoin unique doesn't matter. Make no mistake, all spam on the timechain makes humanity's best attempt at global fair money worse for everyone forever, and not fighting it is enabling it. Putting spam on the timechain is nothing less than an attack on humanity, and anyone engaged in it is either a moron or a sociopath. Bitcoin is robust, but only to the extent that its participants are willing to take responsibility for their actions. Ironically, the same dynamic is true for freedom in general — you can't have it unless you're willing to take responsibility for your life.

Taking responsibility for your life means realizing what life cards you have on hand and starting to play them to the best of your ability. So, what is the goal of the game? Well, that's entirely up to you! Regardless of your game, if you play your cards correctly in each moment, you'll have a better hand to play in the future. Bitcoin is like the Joker card. You can exchange the Joker for any other card at any point, and the further into the game you are, the more powerful this ability becomes.

As long as the world around you stays relatively stable, acquiring a better hand of cards is easy — just avoid spending your satoshis. The real test of your resolve comes the day patience is no longer an option. Whenever the "and then they fight you" phase actually begins, you must choose which side of history you're on, and there are only two options — the Bitcoin maximalist or the nationalist/socialist side. There is no second-best ideology.

Ask yourself: Would you prefer a pro-Bitcoin or an anti-Bitcoin political leader in your country? The answer may seem simple, but this question has more depth than you might think. A pro-bitcoin leader would make life easy for bitcoiners, who might become complacent as a result. In such a scenario, people could forget the importance of running a node, the "not your keys, not your coins" mentality, and many other core Bitcoin principles. Remember that a politician can never give you a right, only take it away.

On the flip side, using Bitcoin properly (privately and securely) is the only option people have in a country with an anti-bitcoin leader. So which one is preferable? The best scenario of them all would be if no human claimed the right to rule another altogether, but it seems unlikely that anyone alive today will ever get a chance to experience such a world. Only by using Bitcoin privately and securely do you have the option to live your life as if politicians didn't have any power over you since if you do, they don't.

It's all noise, and you're better off without it — material cravings, power, attention, political or religious allegiances, beliefs in the supernatural or "the science." Rid yourself of it all. Only then can you be truly free. Reclaim the driver's seat of your life at all costs. Anything less is serfdom. That which you can do without, you own.

EXCELSIOR

Time is money and money's time
We wasted every second dime
On diets, lawyers, shrinks and apps, and flags and plastic surgery.

"So Long, and Thanks for All the Fish"
A Perfect Circle

Clown World is a byproduct of people acting childish and not taking responsibility for their lives. Taking responsibility is what being an adult is all about. As children, we instinctively know that the bully threatening other kids at the playground is a bad actor. Still, we acquiesce to his demands and hand over our toys if he scares us enough. But we know, deep inside, that what he's doing is wrong and that his actions make recess miserable for everyone. As we grow up, we tend to forget that the same "I'm gonna take your stuff, or else . . ." mentality is everywhere. After all, the school itself was probably paid for with lunch money stolen from your parents. It is hard to see the extent of the long-term damage of letting the bullies win.

Preventing bullies from winning requires each individual to take responsibility for their life and actions. Shouting at the system to fix itself and give out more free lunches accomplishes nothing. On the contrary, raging against the machine actually strengthens it, as the eponymous rap-metal band so blatantly exemplifies: "Fuck you, audience; I *will* do what they tell me!"

The only alternative to obedience is responsibility, the flipside of the freedom coin. Eventually, the journey toward taking responsibility will demand that you dissect and comprehend all the implications of succumbing to veiled threats of violence. The not-too-obvious, hidden-in-plain-sight tool for analyzing violence is the price signal.

The enduring principle that prices in a free market gravitate towards the marginal cost of production is as relevant as ever. In an ideally competitive market, one utterly devoid of forceful interventions, the selling price for a product or service will eventually align with the cost of producing one additional unit. Technological progress radically accelerates this trend[1].

Automation, digitalization, and advancements in logistics and manufacturing technologies allow businesses to produce all goods and services at an ever-decreasing cost per unit. Theoretically, this efficiency gain translates into lower consumer prices, facilitating an even more competitive market environment. Moreover, technology opens up access to markets, breaking down the barriers to entry that once protected established firms from new competitors. Conclusion: everything ought to be cheaper, more awesome,

---

1. For more on this topic, read *The Price of Tomorrow* by Jeff Booth.

and more abundant everywhere indefinitely. With increasing downward price pressures, how do we explain why most consumer prices rise? Let's revisit Clown World for a moment!

Market interventions, in general, and government regulations, in particular, hinder technological deflation's ability to improve everyone's lives. By complicating the entrepreneur's life, they stifle innovation. Entrepreneurs, for the most part, comply with regulations voluntarily but not necessarily with consent. Therefore, regulations not only increase costs to the population but also concentrate control. In short, the bureaucracy is expanding to meet the needs of the expanding bureaucracy, leading to higher barriers to entry, artificial monopolies, and, ultimately, Clown World galore.

In Clown World, large corporations lobby for regulatory barriers to protect their interests. This is, of course, a losing battle tactic against the inexorable trend of falling prices. From a Prisoner's Dilemma perspective, these corporations are defectors, not cooperators. They do *not* follow the Tit-for-Tat strategy. But why? Cooperators eventually outcompete defectors, don't they? Yes, this would be true if the system *actually worked*. But the money is broken. In a world where inflation is everywhere, everyone's incentivized to shorten their time horizons and grab as much for themselves as possible before the money loses its value. Clown World results in Tits-for-Tate rather than Tit-for-Tat.

The cost of producing a line of code is virtually nil. In this brave new world, the marginal cost of all digital products and services trends towards, you guessed it, the marginal cost of an addi[illegible] nit. What's the marginal cost of an extra line of [illegible] ght, zero. Unhampered, the friendly forces of a [illegible] narket in the Internet age will usher in an era [illegible] abundance for everyone at breakneck speed. [illegible] to-peer Bitcoin economy, entirely outside the banking system, there are no market interventions to distort the money.

When a currency's value diminishes, holding money becomes less attractive for individuals and investors, prompting them to use assets as a store of value rather than cash. As consumer prices increase, each currency unit buys fewer goods and services, which is particularly detrimental to the poor but also to savers and fixed-income earners as the purchasing power of their stored wealth and future income decline over time. Inflation is wage deflation — the flipside of the same deteriorating coin. On the other hand, a steady Bitcoin income becomes more valuable over time, not less. In Bitcoin, the first million is the easiest, not the hardest.

A bank balance on a computer screen is as sensitive to corrosion as a copper coin in nitric acid. Real estate, stocks, and precious metals have thus replaced the malfunctioning government-issued currencies as media of exchange over time. Neither real estate, stocks, or precious metals are finite, though. The only thing making them suitable as stores of value is their relative scarcity compared to the lack thereof in fiat currencies. Increased asset accumulation diverts resources from productive economic activities, inevitably leading to bubbles in asset markets and increased financial instability. The irony is that individual efforts to safeguard personal wealth, such as investing in seemingly stable assets, reinforce the system and are thus counterproductive.

The results are bifurcated. Those with disposable income can take on debt and purchase assets that increase in value and protect against inflation. Those who don't have assets or disposable income effectively pay for this increase since the only reason assets go up in price is that the purchasing power of the banknotes diminishes. All the while, everyone has t pay for stuff just to survive, regardless of increasing pr or anyone's decreasing ability to pay for said stuff. Inflation thus funnels wealth from the have-nots to the haves at an ever-accelerating pace, and the only handbrake available to reverse the process is absolutely finite money.

Denominated in real money (Bitcoin), it is easy to see that 99.9% of all assets fall in price over enough time. A house is, first and foremost, a consumer good — a thing to live in. Most stocks are overvalued since most companies are zombie companies, and no precious metal is as finite as Element Zero.

Every person living today has experienced nothing but inflationary currencies. The last tie between the dollar and gold was abandoned over fifty years ago, and most people think increasing prices is a natural phenomenon they can do little about. If they only knew what a simple switch to an incorruptible denominator could do to improve their lives. Only through Bitcoin can we genuinely measure the economic shift of prices trending toward marginal production costs and experience the Tit-for-Tat approach as the winning strategy in the game of life. If Bitcoin remains decentralized and secure, all prices across the economy will inevitably decline. The age of abundance would then be upon us.

In a world where value creation is the primary driver of economic activity, government interventions become increasingly obsolete. The role of venture capital also changes dramatically, as investors are forced to focus on continuous innovation and collaboration instead of lobbying and manipulation tactics, as is the case under fiat-based systems. Under a Bitcoin-based economy, power and wealth distribution will be fairer because it will be based on merit, not political connections. The value one provides to society becomes the primary means of earning money, resulting in a continual decrease in marginal costs of production, which will give rise to a more cooperative, abundant, less wasteful, and just world.

Bitcoiners find themselves in a unique position where mutual support is encouraged and incentivized, as all bitcoiners want Bitcoin to succeed. As the value of Bitcoin increases, so do the 'bags' of the hodlers, creating a natural inclination among bitcoiners to be excellent to each other and collaborate as much as possible. It's a synergy where personal gains align with collective benefit. The success of Bitcoin is the success of bitcoiners. They are literally two sides of the same coin. If we were all bitcoiners, we would all be successful.

Funnily enough, the benefits of a Bitcoin-based economy are not limited to the Bitcoin sphere. As productivity increases and both producer and consumer prices fall, even those without any satoshis are better off. Because everything is interconnected, there is no such thing as a circular economy. Even the most stubborn nocoiner stands to gain from the hyperbitcoinization process. You're welcome, Mr. Schiff!

A sound money standard naturally encourages a lower time preference. Such a mindset shifts focus from rampant consumerism to quality-over-quantity thinking. Given a low enough time preference, you eventually figure out that you're playing Prisoner's Dilemma-type games an indefinite number of times. You have all the reasons in the world to cooperate with everyone forever and occasionally punish bad actors justly. In Clown World, where the rules are changed after each game, the long and winding road to success follows obedience, taking on excessive debt, and parroting virtue-signaling mainstream narratives. In Bitcoin, Tit-for-Tat *is* the winning strategy.

Personal hyperbitcoinization also introduces a paradigm shift in the concept of competition. Since all "owning"

Bitcoin requires is the ability to keep a secret, the satoshis literally reside within their owners' brains, making theft, coercion, and violence aimed at bitcoiners way less profitable. If you kill a bitcoiner, you kill their bitcoins, too. Shifting incentives will push people toward more positive-sum catallactic competition and away from fang-and-claw biological competition, where the most aggressive competitor usually wins. In a free market, catallactic competition favors whoever can provide their fellow humans with the best, most price-worthy goods and services, ultimately benefiting all participants.

Bitcoin offers a beacon of hope, illuminating a path to reverse the process of wealth funneling via inflation. Awareness is the first step towards this financial exodus. Once you recognize the fundamental issues plaguing the traditional monetary system, you can voluntarily opt out and transition to the new system.

Bitcoin offers an inversion of the current centrally planned, controlled economic structure — the Inverse of Clown World. In Bitcoin, the wealth created by ever-increasing productivity is distributed among everyone, not concentrated in the hands of a few bureaucrats. Everyone on Earth is better off because an alternative financial system exists, but only those who consciously decide to adopt it to its full extent will enjoy its more profound philosophical benefits. By shifting your focus and resources to anything related to Bitcoin, you contribute to the development of a more just and sustainable world. This transition represents more than just switching to a new type of money; it's a fundamental shift towards a financial paradigm that values truth above all else. In Bitcoin, the cost of trying to cheat the system always far exceeds the cost of playing by the rules, which creates a base layer of truth for all interhuman activities. But it does require you to act.

All of the responsibility is yours and yours only. You must decide how to interact with the Bitcoin network and to which extent you trust the individuals and companies involved. Whether you entrust a custodian to hold your satoshis for you, keep them on a hardware device, or run a node to verify incoming transactions is entirely up to you. Bitcoin management is not a one-size-fits-all proposition. You must decide what works best for you.

Most people aren't accustomed to this level of personal responsibility. People are used to trusting third parties for practically all forms of ownership, which is one of the root causes of fiat systemic rot. The urge for there to be a free lunch undermines everything.

Fiat currencies are credit. They are claims on goods that don't exist. The world has more than 300 trillion dollars of debt, and the only way the fiat system can ease the burden of that debt is to debase the value of money, creating even more debt in the process. One trillion one-dollar bills, laid end to end, would stretch about 96,906,656 miles — further than the distance between the Earth and the sun.

The only way to end the destruction is to stop feeding the beast. Every time you use a fiat currency, you're stealing from your kids. You reinforce the institutions that cause the problem. Every time you use Bitcoin instead, you remove the value of that transaction from these parasitic institutions and simultaneously fertilize the new system. Bitcoin is still just a footnote compared to the enormous fiat economy, but its minuscule size means that the opportunities it presents are unimaginably massive. We are so early it hurts.

Clown World is a byproduct of people not taking responsibility. You achieve the inverse of Clown World through self-reflection and debugging your mental software. Taking responsibility for your actions is the only thing that can make the whole damn circus disappear, on a personal level and a societal one. Become the anti-clown. Become Bitcoin. Excelsior!

POSTFACE

The more you give yourself to Bitcoin, the more of itself it gives back to you, literally and metaphorically. After quitting my fiat job and deciding to devote my life to Bitcoin education, my family and I moved down to our holiday home in Spain. A few weeks after we arrived, Jeff Booth and his family visited us for dinner. I greatly admire Jeff, and having him over for dinner was just as much a surprise as an honor. At some point during the evening, he asked me what my plans for the future were. I shrugged and said, "Selling books and merch, I guess." Jeff looked me right in the eye and replied, "You're not a t-shirt salesman," suggesting I should aim for higher goals.

About a year (and a dozen conferences) later, I met Luke through Konsensus Network, the publishing house I was collaborating with at the time. We decided to start a podcast together, and on Infinity Day 2022, the Freedom Footprint Show was born. A year later, we decided to go completely independent, and now, a year after that, we've written a book together and rebranded the show to the Bitcoin Infinity Show. The ideas in this book are based on our conversations during the Freedom Footprint years.

Luke and I discuss tactics and ethics almost every day and often ask ourselves why we do what we do. The main reason is simple — we want to build relationships with other bitcoiners. Sure, having a ton of subscribers is nice, but we're not in this for attention. We want to live the meme and experience hyperbitcoinization from a front-row seat among friends.

Since we almost always have the same opinion about practically everything, we've decided to expand our collaboration beyond the pod, which is why this book is now a joint venture rather than a solo effort. Our mind-meld is almost scary sometimes, despite our somewhat different but highly compatible skill sets and personality traits. I am a scatterbrained idea machine; Luke is diligent and organized. Every now and then in life, you find people you absolutely love working with. I've experienced such matches just a handful of times. With Luke, the difference is that I now work on stuff I absolutely love doing, which was not necessarily the case back in my fiat career.

This book is the product of that enthusiastic workaholics-not-so-anonymous relationship. After about a hundred podcast episodes, I knew I had another Bitcoin book in me, and one fine day, the material just started pouring out. Because of Luke, the texts are now not just random ideas piled onto one another, which is more or less accurate for my previous works. Instead, there now exists a coherent book with a story structure and twelve strong chapters that can be read as standalone articles if necessary. Without Luke, that would not be the case. I am very proud of what we've managed to squeeze out of our psyches and keyboards together.

"The surreal doesn't end" is a phrase Luke and I often use to describe the feeling we get when we end up in situations where we get to hang out with our bitcoiner friends and idols and form new bonds in idyllic parts of the world. Neither of us intends to stop attending Bitcoin events any time soon. On the contrary, we look forward to getting around as much as possible and befriending as many of you guys as possible. The opportunities in this community are as endless as the rabbit hole is bottomless.

I hope you've enjoyed reading this book as much as we enjoyed writing it, and I can't wait to dissect the ideas in it with each and every one of you, online or in person!

Your fellow pile of sats,
Knut Svanholm
July 2024
A one-horse town in Sweden

Thanks for reading!
For more from Knut and Luke, check out the
Bitcoin Infinity Show!
bitcoininfinityshow.com

Made in the USA
Middletown, DE
21 October 2024

62573732R00099